The Experiences of Muslim Women Employed in the Tourism Industry

Lubna Al Mazro'ei

The Experiences of Muslim Women Employed in the Tourism Industry

The Case of Oman

LAP LAMBERT Academic Publishing

Impressum/Imprint (nur für Deutschland/ only for Germany)

Bibliografische Information der Deutschen Nationalbibliothek: Die Deutsche Nationalbibliothek verzeichnet diese Publikation in der Deutschen Nationalbibliografie; detaillierte bibliografische Daten sind im Internet über http://dnb.d-nb.de abrufbar.

Alle in diesem Buch genannten Marken und Produktnamen unterliegen warenzeichen-, marken- oder patentrechtlichem Schutz bzw. sind Warenzeichen oder eingetragene Warenzeichen der jeweiligen Inhaber. Die Wiedergabe von Marken, Produktnamen, Gebrauchsnamen, Handelsnamen, Warenbezeichnungen u.s.w. in diesem Werk berechtigt auch ohne besondere Kennzeichnung nicht zu der Annahme, dass solche Namen im Sinne der Warenzeichen- und Markenschutzgesetzgebung als frei zu betrachten wären und daher von jedermann benutzt werden dürften.

Coverbild: www.ingimage.com

Verlag: LAP LAMBERT Academic Publishing AG & Co. KG
Dudweiler Landstr. 99, 66123 Saarbrücken, Deutschland
Telefon +49 681 3720-310, Telefax +49 681 3720-3109
Email: info@lap-publishing.com

Herstellung in Deutschland:
Schaltungsdienst Lange o.H.G., Berlin
Books on Demand GmbH, Norderstedt
Reha GmbH, Saarbrücken
Amazon Distribution GmbH, Leipzig
ISBN: 978-3-8383-9186-1

Imprint (only for USA, GB)

Bibliographic information published by the Deutsche Nationalbibliothek: The Deutsche Nationalbibliothek lists this publication in the Deutsche Nationalbibliografie; detailed bibliographic data are available in the Internet at http://dnb.d-nb.de.

Any brand names and product names mentioned in this book are subject to trademark, brand or patent protection and are trademarks or registered trademarks of their respective holders. The use of brand names, product names, common names, trade names, product descriptions etc. even without a particular marking in this works is in no way to be construed to mean that such names may be regarded as unrestricted in respect of trademark and brand protection legislation and could thus be used by anyone.

Cover image: www.ingimage.com

Publisher: LAP LAMBERT Academic Publishing AG & Co. KG
Dudweiler Landstr. 99, 66123 Saarbrücken, Germany
Phone +49 681 3720-310, Fax +49 681 3720-3109
Email: info@lap-publishing.com

Printed in the U.S.A.
Printed in the U.K. by (see last page)
ISBN: 978-3-8383-9186-1

Copyright © 2010 by the author and LAP LAMBERT Academic Publishing AG & Co. KG and licensors
All rights reserved. Saarbrücken 2010

Dedication

This book is dedicated to my husband, my son and my parents for their love, support and encouragement throughout the duration of my research.

Table of Contents

Dedication..i
Table of Contents...ii
Chapter 1: Introduction..1
    Author's Background Information..2
Chapter 2: Literature Review..4
    The Status of Muslim Women in the Middle East: Historic Influences and
    Recent Changes..4
        Religion and culture..5
        Male domination..6
        Literacy and education..7
        Stereotypes...7
        The potential for change in Muslim women's status.....................9
    Muslim Women and Employment...10
        Issues surrounding employment patterns for Muslim Women...............10
        Explanations for low employment and unemployment rates for
        Muslim women..11
        The potential for growth in Muslim women employment: Opportunities
        and constraints through tourism employment..............................13
        Issues surrounding tourism employment for Muslim women...............15
    Summary...17
Chapter 3: The Research Process..20
    The Research Site...20
    Theoretical Paradigm...25
    Using Grounded Theory...26
    Recruitment and Participants..27
    Information About The Women..28
    Data Collection...29
    Data Analysis...31
        Initial coding...31
        Focused coding...32
        Theoretical coding..32

    Validation and Presentation of Findings..33
    Ethical Issues...33

Chapter 4: Findings..35
    Theme 1: Finding Work in the Tourism Field..35
        1.1 Choosing tourism as a career choice...35
        1.2 Dealing with job access difficulties..36
        1.3 Needing particular skills, personalities and attitudes.....................37
    Theme 2: Facing Negative Attitudes..39
        2.1 Employer's attitudes...39
        2.2 Society's attitudes..40
        2.3 Family members' attitudes...41
        2.4 Husband's attitudes..42
        2.5 Women's self attitudes..43
    Theme 3: Challenges of Tourism Work...46
        3.1 The challenges of work conditions and demands.........................46
        3.2 The challenges of progressing in tourism work............................48
        3.3 The challenges of being a working wife and mother.....................49
        3.4 The challenge of discrimination against local employees..............50
        3.5 The challenge of being in the front line......................................51
        3.6 The challenge of low pay...52
    Theme 4: Dealing with Negative Attitudes and Challenges.................................53
        4.1 Accepting, adapting and finding strategies to address challenges.......53
        4.2 Making choices with regard to child related issues.......................55
        4.3 Accepting and conforming to employers' and societal attitudes........56
        4.4 Attempting to change family members' and husbands' attitudes......57
    Theme 5: Importance of Tourism Work in Women's lives.................................59
        5.1 Enjoying tourism work..59
        5.2 Learning new skills..60
        5.3 Increased strength, confidence, independence and status................62
        5.4 Having life changing experience..64
    Theme 6: An Expanded Vision of Tourism Work...64
        6.1 Gaining a broader perspective of tourism work............................64
        6.2 Increased tourism development opportunities in Oman.................65

    6.3 Increased opportunities for women..67
    6.4 The need for better training and resources...................................69
  Theme 7: Implications for Social Change..71
    7.1 The importance of career success..71
    7.2 Challenging traditional attitudes..72
  Summary..73

Chapter 5: Discussion and Conclusion..75

  Emergent Themes...75
  Tourism Work as Exploitation of Women...78
    Low paid and unskilled work...78
    Limited career advancement..78
    Working hours..79
    Societal and cultural barriers...79
  Tourism Work as Empowerment for Women...80
    Fun and enjoyment..81
    Learning new skills..81
    Gaining confidence, independence and status...................................81
    Empowerment..82
  Tourism as a Source of Social Change...83
    The image of the tourism industry...83
    Tourism as an appropriate employment for women...........................84
    Desire to change attitudes to women in general.................................84
    Resistance to cultural attitudes...85
  Study Significance..86
  Strength and Weaknesses...88
    Social constructionism...88
    Grounded theory..88
    The interviews..89
    Member checks...90
    Sample..90
  Future Directions for Tourism and Research in Oman............................91
  Final Thoughts..92

References..93

Chapter 1: Introduction

In many parts of the world, cultural and religious expectations have led to low rates of workforce participation among Muslim women. However, Muslim women today are playing an increasing role in the workforce despite these expectations. One of the reasons for the expansion of female employment is the growing number of jobs available for women. For example, the rapid growth of the tourism industry in many parts of the world has led to an increase in the number of jobs deemed to be appropriate for women (Ghodsee, 2003; Liu & Wall, 2006; Mansfeld & Winckler, 2008).

A growing body of literature (e.g., Small, 1999) has examined the role that the tourism industry plays in the lives of women employees. These studies have tended to focus on women in Western countries (Jordan, 1997; Phillimore, 2002;) and developing countries (Bolles, 1997; Cukier, 2002). Both positive and negative aspects of tourism employment have been addressed (e.g., accessibility, seasonality, low status, low pay, and exploitation.). Nevertheless, some satisfaction with this form of employment is evident, particularly among women from developing countries, where employment in tourism is seen to improve women's economic status (Bolles, 1997; Ghodsee, 2003).

Relatively little attention has been paid to the employment of Muslim women in the tourism industry in the Middle East, North Africa or the Arabian Peninsula (Sonmez, 2001). This may be because accurate data are difficult to obtain (Moghadam, 1995). The few studies that have been done have suggested that tourism employment may offer specific opportunities and benefits for Muslim women, such as training opportunities, availability of jobs, access to jobs previously filled by men, etc. (Miles, 2002, Moghadam, 1998; Sonmez, 2001). This suggests that tourism employment might potentially help to improve the status of women in Muslim societies. However, the studies that have explored tourism employment for Muslim women have not addressed problems related to cultural and religious factors, nor have they explored difficulties related to tourism employment. Some authors have discussed the negative stereotypes that are held in western societies about Muslim women, but how this relates specially to tourism employment for Middle Eastern women is not clear (Al Mahadin & Burns, 2007, Gray & Finely-Hervey, 2005).

In general, there remains a lack of information about tourism employment for Muslim women, particularly in the Middle East. It is important to bridge this gap in the literature in order to provide a better understanding of modern Muslim women working in the tourism industry. Moreover, there is clearly a need to understand Muslim women's employment roles in different cultural and societal settings. This would help to identify the commonalities and differences among the world's women and to increase cross-cultural understanding. It might also help to eliminate western stereotypes about

Muslim women by gaining some insight into the potential for tourism employment to positively influence the status of women in Muslim societies. Bolles (1997) argues that research on women in the tourism industry could strengthen the idea of women as competent hosts and workers in the tourism industry and enhance understanding of the effects that tourism has on the local female population. This kind of research may be particularly important in Muslim societies, for example in the Middle East, were little research has been conducted to date on this topic.

The purpose of this study is to understand the experiences and meanings of tourism employment for Muslim women in the Middle East, including the positive and negative aspects of this form of employment. The study uses qualitative interviews to understand the perspectives of Muslim women employed in this industry. Specifically, it addresses the following questions:

- How do Muslim women in Oman experience working in the tourism industry?
- What does it mean to these women to work in the tourism industry?
- What are the benefits of tourism employment in Oman as perceived by Muslim women employees?
- What difficulties do these employees encounter through tourism employment due to cultural, religious and other constraints?
- What is the overall impact of tourism employment on the lives of Muslim women?

Although the Middle East shares certain commonalities in terms of religion and cultural ideologies towards women, it should be noted that women's experiences are diversified because of the variety of socio-economic, political and cultural arrangements in different Middle Eastern countries. Therefore, it was important to select a particular cultural setting for this study; as Moghadam (2003) says, "to study the Middle East and Middle Eastern women is to recognize the diversity within the region and within the female population" (p.10). In order to provide credible information about Muslim women employed in the tourism industry, this study focuses on women in Oman. Oman was deemed to be an appropriate location for this study because of the growth of the tourism industry in that country as well as recent government encouragement for women to participate in tourism employment. A thorough discussion about Oman as a research site is presented in the research process chapter.

Overall, the goal for this study was to provide a stepping-stone towards understanding the changing role of Muslim women, and in particular to do this through exploration of the current literature and through the voices of the women that were interviewed.

Author's Background Information

I am a Muslim woman and I am originally from Oman. My interest in this topic occurred during a literature review research that I was undertaking for one of my master's degree course reports, which addressed the dynamics of tourism in Islamic societies. The particular literature that led me to undertake my study topic was a paper by Sonmez (2001) titled "Tourism behind the veil of Islam: Women and development in the Middle East". In this paper, Sonmez (2001) discusses tourism development in the Middle East and the involvement of Muslim women in tourism employment. However, the information on this topic was limited, a common problem found in this area of tourism research.

Because I am passionate about the tourism industry and being a Muslim woman, I wanted to explore Muslim women's experiences and meanings in tourism employment, including both the benefits and constraints of tourism employment for Muslim women. There are many negative perceptions held about Muslim women, largely I believe, due to biases in the media and other sources. However, I hoped to reveal, through my research, that Muslim women are prospering and are playing a major role in the workforce. I also hoped to provide new insight into the lives of modern Muslim women. Oman was chosen as the research site for my study, not only because I am originally from Oman, but also because I wanted to explore the experiences of Omani women working in an industry that is still growing. Being a Muslim woman, with a background in tourism, I hoped to reveal how religion and tourism influence the lives of Muslim women such as myself, and to include the voices of other Muslim women working in the tourism industry. Through this brief introduction about my perspective and myself, I hope to provide an understanding of the overall purpose of my study and my motivation for choosing this particular research topic.

Chapter 2: Literature Review

The purpose of the literature review is to showcase the various issues that are affecting Muslim women in the Middle East and the current opportunities that are arising for them. The first section of the literature review looks into the status of Muslim women in the Middle East in order to provide an understanding of the various religious and cultural constraints that Muslim women encounter in their everyday life. However, there is a potential for change in Muslim women's status despite the cultural and religious constraints. In other words, there are increasing opportunities for Muslim women to contribute to society, particularly through their contribution to paid work. Although change is taking place, this section of the literature review also reveals that there are several constraints that still persist, which may make social change difficult.

As the focus of the study is on tourism employment for Muslim women, the following section of the chapter will focus on Muslim women and employment in terms of employment patterns and rates for Muslim women. Although this section reveals the various difficulties that Muslim women encounter with respect to access to employment, it also indicates that there are opportunities opening up for Muslim women, especially in the tourism industry. However, religious and cultural constraints are still in existence, which may make it difficult for Muslim women to work in this particular industry. In order to further understand opportunities and constraints of tourism employment for Muslim women, the literature review then leads into a discussion of the issues surrounding tourism employment for Muslim women. The positive and negative aspects of tourism employment for women in general are addressed. Specific issues that Muslim women may encounter due to cultural and religious concerns are also detailed.

Finally, a summary of the literature review is provided at the end, which summarizes the main points made in the literature review and leads into the discussion of the research process chapter. Overall, the literature review supports the potential value of the research and indicates the need to fill the literature gap in the area of Muslim women's development.

The Status of Muslim Women in the Middle East: Historic Influences and Recent Changes

In order to understand the issue of Muslim women in tourism employment, it is important to consider their status in society in general. This was emphasized by Sonmez (2001) when she argued that issues of gender equity and women's economic and political contribution in the Middle East should be understood in terms of the broader environment that is characterized by patriarchal society, Middle Eastern culture and Islam. Furthermore, Sonemz (2001) argues that there is a need to evaluate

Middle Eastern countries' development levels and the status of women in those societies, as it is clear that women are not utilized fully as potential human resources for their countries.

According to Baden (1992), different approaches have been taken in addressing women's status in Muslim countries by writers from different backgrounds. Further, it is clear that the study of women's status in Muslim countries is controversial because of the history of tensions between Eurocentric views and anti-Western views. For example, writers such as Kandiyoti (1991) focus on the state, its relationship and responses to political movements (which includes political Islam and feminism) and on the international political and economic context. Due to the increasing influence of Islamic fundamentalists, other studies, for example, Ahmed (as cited in Baden, 1992) and Keddie and Baron (1991) have focused on the evolution of discourses on women within Islam, women's private and public roles, and their struggles through modern history. A variety of influences on the status of Muslim women are evident in the literature, including religion, culture, male domination, literacy, education and stereotypes.

Religion and culture.

The status of women in Muslim societies is highly influenced by religion and by the cultural interpretation of Islam. It is a common western view that the status of women is worse in Muslim countries compared to other countries. This is thought to be linked to the dominant role that Islam plays in these societies with regard to issues such as gendered segregation, which is customary and sometimes legally enforced, and to the view of Muslim women as primarily wives and mothers. Although Islamic teaching does allow women to work for pay, all economic provision is thought to be the responsibility of men; women are expected to marry and produce children in order to gain status. In most Muslim countries, women must receive consent from their husbands, fathers or brothers in order to work. The conduct of Muslim women is very much controlled, in part because of the focus on maintaining family honor and a good reputation, and to avoid the negative consequences of shame. This view of women's role is reflected in data reported during the late 1980's that showed that 34% of all brides in Muslim countries were under the age of 20 when they married and women in Muslim countries bore an average of six children (Moghadam, 2003).

Although Muslim women do have rights within the Islamic religion, as emphasized in the Quran (Islam holy book), the Hadith (the sayings of the prophet Mohammed), Shariah (Islamic law) and fiqh (rules), according to Islam-Husain (as cited in Sonmez, 2001), many cultural biases skew individual and collective interpretations, distorting the Quran specifications. Sonmez (2001) claims that women are permitted to work outside their home as long as they dress modestly and do not neglect their families. Unfortunately, women's participation in the work force is often forbidden by their male relatives. Also, although Islamic teachings grant women the rights to earnings, property and wealth, women's earnings are often given directly to their husbands and fathers. Furthermore, while Islamic teaching does give women the right to financial security and inheritance, again many women are denied their inheritances and are thus dependent on their male relatives for financial security (Sonmez, 2001).

Sonmez (2001) argues that Islam influences all aspects of life in Muslim societies. Thus Islam is not only a religious influence, but also deeply embedded within all aspects of the culture of Islamic societies. Accordingly, the problems that women face in terms of achievement of economic independence can be seen as both cultural and religious, and Islamic culture is a major force affecting women's human rights and the possibilities of progressive social transformation. This view was also emphasized by Nga-Longva who claims that there is a "general tendency to assess women's opportunities and constraints in terms of what the Quran and Islamic tradition dictate, not in terms of secular and more immediate concerns they may share with the rest of society"(as cited in Sonmez, 2001 p. 127). This, in turn, is underscored by the assumptions that Muslim women are not part of society in general and that their lives remain unaffected by any change occurring around them. Thus, Islam-Husain (as cited in Sonmez, 2001) suggests that it is not surprising that Muslim women's rights, as outlined in Islamic religious texts, are not necessarily honored in Islamic societies. Furthermore, the idea that men have higher legal status than women perpetuates the social barriers and constraints that women face in terms of achievements outside the family environment. Islamic culture also places emphasis on the fundamental differences between men and women and the special care that has to be exercised in order to avoid women's participation in "inappropriate roles". Overall, these assumptions and beliefs have been used as justification for gender segregation in public, women's restriction to the home, and women's lack of civil and legal rights (Moghadam, 2003).

Male domination.

Women's position in Islamic societies is usually characterized as one of being dominated by men. Gray and Finely-Hervey (2005) describe women as being "viewed to be docile without any capacity or contribution to debate or commercial society" (p.204). This relationship of domination contradicts the fundamental tenets of Islam (equal rights, duties and opportunities of education) of political and cultural participation and contribution for women. Thus, the problem would appear to lie mostly with the men, men's perspectives and with cultural imperatives rather than with religion per se, as the Quran encourages equal opportunities for men and women in education, political participation rights and duties. Despite the encouragement of equality of men and women in the Quran, Glasse (1989) does point out that the Quran ascribes different social roles to men and women based on their perceived different natures. So this may also have contributed to perception of strict roles for women about what is deemed to be appropriate social behaviors. In Islamic society, men are seen as the providers and protectors of the family. For example, Howard-Merriam (1990) states "men are the protectors and maintainers of women, because God has given the one more (strength) than the other and because they support them from their means" (p.18). Furthermore, in Islamic society, women have two minority statues, that is, they are under the guardianship of their father or elder brothers before marriage, and under the protection of their husbands following marriage (Baden, 1992). The domination of men in Arab societies has been perceived as being anachronistic and grossly authoritarian. Media representations and western literature often reflect men's domination of women in these societies.

Literacy and education.

Literacy rates for women in the Middle East and North Africa are quite low in comparison to more developed nations. Due to the low literacy level that women have in the Middle East, women may lack awareness about human rights. Also women's educational levels in Arab nations are further constrained by high fertility rates. That is, when there is a high rate of fertility, women are less likely to be literate and unlikely to work outside the home (Sonmez, 2001). Furthermore, the influence of family law in the region has had an impact on women's ability to make independent decisions affecting their personal and economic lives due to their lack of education. Although specific aspects of family law differ from country to country in the region, in general, the law remains a primary force that resists feminist attempts to reform (Doumato & Poususney, 2003).

Thus, Sonmez (2001) concludes that gender differences in literacy rates reflect unequal access to education as well as differences in power and social valuation. Sonmez (2001) notes that many uneducated women are confined and unable to access paid employment because of bearing and looking after children at home and because of lack of education. On the other hand, educated women are also constrained and denied their legal rights when they are unable to find well paying jobs.

Stereotypes.

Some of the problems that women face in Islamic cultures are known about in Western societies too. While these problems may be "accepted" by Westerners as an inevitable aspect of Middle Eastern life, they also lead to stereotyping of Islamic culture and negative perceptions of Muslim women. These negative views and stereotypes are usually informed by an "oriental's" perspective, according to Said (1978, 1993). One of these stereotypes is that Muslim women are "weak, capricious and untrustworthy creatures, who tends to be ruled by [their] 'instincts' and whose powerful sexuality, if left uncontrolled, can cause distortion and social chaos" (Rassam as cited in Gray & Finely-Hervey, 2005, p.205). Another stereotype is that Muslim women are always oppressed. Although this is true in some Islamic societies, this stereotype, by definition, is not universally applicable. One of Pope's (as cited in Gray & Finely-Hervey, 2005, p.205) respondents in a study of professional Muslim women from Saudi Arabia said, " [it's] rubbish that we're oppressed. I've lived both here and in the west, so I should know". The same participant acknowledged that "there are restrictions and you work around them. Discretion is the name of the game". Thus, although this negative stereotype of Muslim women does reflect reality for many women, as discussed, it is not true for all Muslim women since some are able to fight for personal freedom, education and opportunities for employment.

Similarly, the inaccurate perception that Muslim women are submissive is often based on women dressing from head to toe in black. Although there are women in the Middle East who do live a very strict life such as wearing a burka, not working, not driving and not traveling without permission, Sonmez (2001) says that there are many women in the region who live a lifestyle that is similar to western women. For example, women in Egypt are increasingly involved in their country's workforce. Some women in Cyprus, Turkey and Israel also have high levels of equality and participate in the workforce. However, these educated working women are the exceptions rather than the rule, so socioeconomic indicators do not indicate widespread (or general) change in levels of education or employment.

Despite the many issues that affect women's status in Muslim societies, Seiklay (1994) cautions that each Muslim woman's experience is different and that experiences vary from one country to another. These differences between cultures also suggest that Western perceptions are based on overgeneralized stereotypes. For example, Western observers hear about difficulties that women in one country experience, and then assume that this applies to all Muslim countries. However, each country has its own climate and level of tolerance for increased empowerment of women. Furthermore, as discussed earlier, the blame does not lie on Islam per se, nor is Islam different in many regards from other religions such as Hinduism, Judaism and Christianity, which share the common traditional views of women as wives and mothers. Thus, the gender-powered relations that govern women's status are not unique to Muslims or to Middle Eastern countries, since they can be found in other countries as well. For example, religious based law exists in the Jewish state of Israel, high fertility rates were common in western countries in the early stage of industrialization, and in western societies women were disadvantaged in terms of occupational opportunities until fairly recently (Moghadam, 2003).

Overall, though, when looking at the status of Muslim women in the Middle East, Alvi (2005) notes that it can be seen that there has been a failure to empower women. Women in this region have endured a long battle fighting to achieve equality, to gain economic and political empowerment, and to achieve higher standards of living and quality of life. For example, in 2000, literacy rates for women in Oman were at 46% and 50% in Saudi Arabia. Furthermore, female economic activity rates were at

8.7% in Oman and 18.9% in Saudi Arabia (Central Intelligence Agency, as cited in Sonmez, 2001). As discussed earlier, Muslim social customs are based on the societal and familial dominance of males as well as Islamic cultures that prohibit the mingling of different sexes in public. This makes it difficult for Muslim women to be part of business transactions in a Muslim culture. However, Gray and Finely-Hervey (2005) emphasize that there is an emerging trend for Muslim women to bypass many rules and regulations by pursuing entrepreneurship opportunities. Gray and Finely-Hervey's (2005) study of women and entrepreneurship in Morocco notes that many Muslim women have been able to overcome the male dominance in that country by pursuing entrepreneurship opportunities and by establishing businesses independent of males. Thus, at least in some societies, change seems to be occurring which is leading to new opportunities for Muslim women. These changes will be discussed in the next section.

The potential for change in Muslim women's status.

Based on the previous discussion, it is evident that Muslim women's status has a major impact on their access to employment. However, this situation may be changing due to globalization and modernization. According to Doumato and Posusney (2003), globalization is closely interrelated with the evolving role of women in the Middle East. This, they claim, will lead to shifts in societal attitudes toward gender and affect women's opportunities for employment. That is, the values of many Arab and Muslim countries are being challenged and gradually transformed and replaced.

The new values incorporate many western perspectives, which include increased employment opportunities for women. There are both negative and positive outcomes of this change for Muslim women and Muslim societies. For those women who choose an independent path despite religion, socio-economic and legal obstacles, personal success and achievements are sometimes possible. However, these women risk being resented in their society due to their increased independence (Gray & Finely-Hervey, 2005). Also, although the changes are encouraging in many ways, Sonmez (2001) notes the numbers of employed women are still very low when compared to developed nations. Thus gender equity and societal development is slow and sometimes contradictory. For example, based on the AHDR (Arab Human Development Report) survey results on the empowerment of women, Arab respondents were ranked third in rejecting the idea that a university education is more important for a boy than for a girl, while at the same time, Arabs expressed the highest agreement with the idea that when jobs are scarce, men should have more right to a job than women. In other words, "Arabs stood for gender equality in education but not in employment" (as cited in Alvi, 2005 p.156).

Alvi (2005) states, "most of the Arab/Islamic world is characterized by coexisting religious and political authoritarianism, rendering socio-political changes to traditional systems more difficult. In fact, traditions are deeply entrenched, as reflected in the region's social policies" (p.143), which, as discussed before, are based on Islamic culture and particular interpretation of Islam. Because of this, the Arab/Muslim world has struggled to deal with changes due to globalization and modernization throughout the twentieth century and continues to struggle with these issues (Alvi, 2005). This is especially true with respect to the empowerment of women. Alvi (2005) notes that there are forces that exist in the region that reject lifestyle elements of western origin and have attempted to pull the Arab society back into the traditional cultural lifestyle. Thus, Islamic societies have often resisted westernization and the challenges of modernization and globalization. Furthermore, Muslim women's status is in constant danger of being affected by growing religious fundamentalism, which resists any movement towards women's independence (Sonmez, 2001).

Nevertheless, some changes, if slow, are evident in terms of patterns of women's employment. These, in turn, may have the potential to affect society in general and to influence women's power and status (Curtin as cited in Fordyce, Rhadi, Maurice, Van Arsdol & Deming, 1985). Buvinic (as cited in Fordyce et al, 1985) predicated that these changing patterns might lead to a move towards modernity in society. The World Bank has listed a wide range of positive reasons for supporting women in economic development. One of them is that supporting women would help reduce the gender gap and gender stereotyping of Muslim society. Supporting women would also, they claim, help eliminate old social practices such as early marriage and gender discrimination, and may assist in changing roles in the work force (as cited in Al-Jabi, 2003). Furthermore, Sonmez (2001) argues that it is important to include women in development goals in order to ensure gender equity and to strengthen societal development.

Overall, it can be seen that there is a potential for change for Muslim women in the Middle East through employment, despite the various influences that constrain their lives. To further assess the possibility of change for Muslim women through employment, the next section will take a more focused approach by looking at employment patterns for Muslim women and emergent employment opportunities that continue to grow despite existing constraints.

Muslim Women and Employment

Issues surrounding employment patterns for Muslim women.

The need to look at human resource capabilities in Muslim societies was argued in the United Nations Development Report on Arab Human Development (as cited in Gray & Finley-Hervey, 2005). The report states "the potential for developing the knowledge capabilities of Arab countries is enormous not only because of their untapped human capital but also because of their rich cultural, linguistic and intellectual heritage" (as cited in Gray & Finley-Hervey, 2005 p.203). However, the issue of women's employment in the Middle East has not been investigated thoroughly. As Miles (2002) states, the issue of women's employment in the Middle East has "not figured prominently in the literature on women's employment and yet it is fertile ground for such an investigation"(p.413).

Miles (2002) points out that studies of women's employment in the Middle East are mostly focused on social and cultural factors that constrains women's participation in the workforce such as "the conservative nature of Islam, the strength of family ties, the definition of the women's role as that of wife and mother, the segregation of women and men to avoid social problems, cultural restrictions on women's mobility, [and] the stigma attached to a husband whose wife works outside the home" (p.414). While there is some truth to this view, such studies perpetuate the negative rather than positive aspects of women's status.

When attempting to assess employment patterns for Muslim women, the accuracy of the official statistics can be a problem. According to Alvi (2005), one of the problems in assessing women's employment rates in the region is the poor and out of date statistics that are available. Based on the AHDR 2002 report (as cited in Alvi, 2005), the gender based employment ratio in the region is unbalanced. For example, in 1997, labor force participation rates for females in Egypt were at 22.1 % in comparison to 51.4% for males. Also labor force participation rates for females in Qatar were at 0% in comparison to 72.0% for males (The AHDR as cited in Alvi, 2005). Moreover, Sonmez (2001) argues, "labor force participation rates do not present a complete picture of women's contribution to their country's economy, mainly because domestic work is not counted and nondomestic work may not be fully reflected"(p.119). Nevertheless, female labor force participation rates in Muslim countries are clearly lower than those in non-Muslim countries for several reasons (Baden, 1992). This will be explained in the next section.

Explanations for low employment and unemployment rates for Muslim women.

Women in non-Muslim countries made up 36.6% of the labor force compared to 21.3% of women in Muslim countries in 1975 (Moghadam, 1992), and this may be due to factors such as male domination and Islamic fundamentalism, rather than Islamic teachings per se. That is, when Muslim women are denied employment through their family members, the problem lies with the tradition, not Islam (Riphenburg, 1998). There is also little systematic evidence that shows Islam as a factor in either demand or supply (Baden, 1992). Furthermore, Papps (1992) noted that participation rates for females in the labor force vary between countries in terms of both the overall level and the distribution of female economic activity across different sectors. This also raises questions about the importance of Islam as an explanatory factor. For example, in Saudi Arabia, there are few women that are economically active due to their circumscribed public lives and women make up less than 5% of the workforce in that country (Goodwin, 2002).

Nevertheless, it can be argued that the generally low rates of women's labor force participation compared to other parts of the world reflects Muslim women's roles in the Middle East, and these roles appear to be closely linked to Islamic laws and societies. This is evident through the social stigma that is attached to women who participate in the labor force, and the fact that employment is not perceived to be part of women's roles (Moghadam, 2003). Further, since bearing children is highly valued in Middle Eastern cultures and since childbearing is seen to be an important aspect of women's lives, pregnancy and care for young children also limit women's opportunities for employment. The lack of available childcare in some countries means that family and domestic chores are also a heavy burden for employed women (Al-Jabi, 2003).

Family honor and the idea of female modesty have also been linked to the restriction on female employment in Arab societies. These cultural values have traditionally restricted and limited women activities to the domestic sphere. In addition, apart from general attitudes to Muslim women's employment, and problems associated with childcare, women who are seeking paid employment face other problems too. For example, there may be a lack of availability of jobs, and those jobs that are available may be limited to particular economic sectors.

Keddie (1991) points out that there have been disagreements in Muslim societies about whether women should be "allowed" to work, in part because of their assumed responsibilities for children and for childcare. This suggests that there is a fear that employment may affect Muslim women's expected role and family responsibilities. The idea of employment contradicts the view of the ideal women as someone who is a wife and mother and who stays at home, cares for her family and raises a new generation of good Muslim children (Doumato & Posusney, 2003). Although this portrayal is idealized by extremists, it is also supported by governments who are facing unemployment problems and want to open up job opportunities for men. Women's domination by men (e.g., Doumato & Posusney, 2003) has contributed to this idealized view.

High unemployment rates in the Middle East also play a role in women's labor participation. For women, the problem is largely one of inability to enter the labor force rather than from being laid off. According to Shaban, Assaad and Al-Qudsi (1995), about 83% of unemployed women are first time jobseekers compared to 55% of unemployed men. The unemployment rate is also more of a problem for young women as unemployment rates are very high for women aged 15-24 years but lower for older women. Shaban et al. (1995) provide several explanations for this gender difference. One is that the Arab female labor force is young and young women withdraw early from the labor force due to marriage or child bearing. Another explanation is that employers may discriminate against women by hiring more men when jobs are limited. Also women and their families may have a cultural preference for work in sectors where employment is not expanding (e.g., certain public sector or formal sector jobs).

The potential for growth in Muslim women employment: Opportunities and constraints through tourism employment.

Despite the various constraints surrounding low employment and unemployment rates for females in the Middle East, there has been a recent growth of female labor force participation rates in the Middle East, primarily due to the higher levels of education for women (Winckler, 2002). Higher employment rates have also been boosted by the availability of government employment for educated women (Shaban et al, 1995). The increase of participation of women in the workforce has resulted in an overall increase of labor force rates in the region (Winckler, 2002), and thus can be seen to have substantially benefited the economy. This increase is mostly concentrated among young educated women working in the public sector (Shaban et al, 1995). For example, female labor participation in Saudi Arabia increased from 4.9% in 1980 to 10.4% in 1997 (International labor office as cited in Winckler, 2002).

There have also been other changes occurring in the region that may have helped to boost female employment rates and open more doors for Muslim women's access to employment. There are several women's voluntary associations that exist in the region for economic, social, religious and educational purposes. Recently, there has also been an increase in locally formed non-governmental organizations, in some places, that are supporting women and their families when there is a lack of employment or social services. For example, these types of support can be found in countries such as Egypt, Algeria and Palestine, where Islamic charitable societies provide daycare for working mothers as well as income subsides for families in need (Doumato & Posusney, 2003).

In terms of specific employment opportunities, encouragement of certain kinds of industrialization, such as tourism, may also be assisting job opportunities for women, as has been seen in the case of Jordan. Chincilla, Lim and Safa (as cited in Miles, 2002) all note that Jordan is seeking to increase its economic activity by focusing on industries such as tourism that hire women. Moghadam (1998) further states that "this seems to be occurring in Tunisia and Morocco, and to a lesser extent in Turkey, Syria and Egypt...Already, hotel management schools in a number of countries are training young women" (p.21). With the growth of the tourism industry in the Middle East, Moghadam (1998) forecasts a growing involvement of women in tourism-related sales and services occupations, which were previously filled by men, as well as the related increase in hotel management schools for women.

Sonmez (2001) suggests, "it would be highly desirable for Middle Eastern women to initiate efforts to take advantage of tourism wage-earning opportunities in order to gain more independence as women do in other parts of the world"(p.133). Studies from other parts of the world also seem to suggest that tourism employment is often attractive to women. For example, Bolles' (1997) study on Jamaican women found that these women were satisfied with their employment in tourism and that they felt they would be worse off if such opportunities did not exist for them. Ghodsee's (2003) study of women and tourism employment in post-socialist Bulgaria concludes that certain economic sectors such as tourism can help improve the relative economic welfare of women.

However, although there are many positive aspects of women employment in tourism as emphasized by Bolles (1997) and Ghodsee (2003), there might also be negative aspects of women's employment in tourism as well. Miles (2002) says that it is not clear whether the simple availability for tourism jobs in Jordan will necessarily help overcome the problems of women's unemployment especially among young educated women. Specifically, for uneducated women in Jordan, she notes,

> Young women do not see opportunities for themselves in the tourism sector, another sector projected to grow under economic restructuring. If jobs begin to open up for women in the tourism sector as the proponents of structural adjustment believe, it is clear there will be a need for public education campaigns to inform young people and their families what the jobs entails and how women can obtain the training to build their competences. Providing information to young women would strengthen their negotiating position within the families and therefore improve their access to and chances in the labor market (p. 425).

Furthermore, Muslim women's access to tourism employment varies within the Middle East. In those countries in the Middle East which have more open societies, such as Turkey, or where tourism is more established and accepted, such as Egypt, women are more likely to work as cleaners, tour guides, receptionists, secretaries, accountants, travel agents, shopkeepers, managers and administrators in the tourism industry. Thus, women's involvement in tourism employment is mostly evident in countries that are open to change (Sonmez, 2001). In the more conservative societies, women's employment in tourism is more limited. For example, based on a study conducted by Sadi and Henderson (2005) on local versus foreign workers in the hospitality and tourism industry in Saudi Arabia, 68% of those surveyed agreed that local Saudi women are not well represented in the hospitality and tourism industry workforce especially at a supervisory level. The authors suggest that the male dominated workforce needs to make room for the entry of women at some stage and that educational institutions restricted to women should be encouraged to introduce hospitality and tourism studies in their curriculum (Sadi & Henderson, 2005). This, in turn, suggests a need to make changes that will encourage Muslim women to work, especially in the tourism industry.

Overall, it can be seen that there is a potential for growth for Muslim women's employment through tourism. However, there are several constraints that may persist and limit tourism employment opportunities. In order to further understand opportunities and constraints of tourism employment for Muslim women, the next section will explore issues surrounding tourism employment for Muslim women, through discussion of the types of tourism jobs available, and some of the positive and negative aspects of these tourism jobs.

Issues surrounding tourism employment for Muslim women.

In the tourism industry, employers usually recruit for particular types of work based on three main elements: labor, price and gender (Swain, 1995). Employment in the tourism industry is often highly gendered (Kinnaird, Kothari, & Hall, 1994) with women and men employed in different job categories (Enloe, 1989; Swain, 1993, 1995). Typically, this gendering of jobs within tourism means that women are more generally found in low-paid subjugated domestic work, service, and handicraft production, and work as clerks, cooks and servers and even commercial sex workers (Enloe, 1989; Swain, 1993, 1995).

This situation of low status positions for women in tourism is evident in both developed and developing nations (Jordan, 1997; Richter as cited in Sonmez, 2001), where many women have seasonal, part-time, lower-skilled and lower paying jobs, and few of these women have access to well paid skilled and managerial positions. Furthermore, Jordan (1997) suggests that women's employment in tourism is both horizontally and vertically segregated, with women found in positions subordinate to males in an occupational hierarchy (Stockdale, 1991). Because of this, Sonmez (2001) suggests that men's dominance in the tourism industry has a direct bearing on the exploitation of women. Moreover, women's position in tourism employment is also influenced by the image of men as travelers and women as hostesses, which "has enabled national governments and tourist organizations to portray women in a service role" (Jordan, p.528, 1997).

The types of jobs that are available to women are not only low status jobs, but also demand stereotypical feminine skills such as cleaning, cooking, so forth, which reflect patriarchal domestic divisions of labor (Swain, 1995). Due to women's concentration in these types of jobs, Swain (1995) argues that this reinforces "male breadwinner/female dependency relations in the home". Furthermore, Burns (1993) argues that women are disproportionately represented in tourism because they are assumed to be dependents of a breadwinner. Employers, it is argued, see women as dependents and men as ambitious. Due to this, women are placed in "feminine" fields and excluded from other fields, which are higher status and better paid. The gendered nature of women's work as being low status and menial also suggests exploitation and sex objectification. While some employers may believe that objectification of women is justified because of the commercial needs of the tourism industry (Jordan, 1997), others would see this as exploitation. In addition, as Scott (1997) notes, "women's choices with regards to tourism employment are circumscribed both by their individual qualifications and experience, and by the social and cultural pressures which apply to women working in the leisure field" (p.66). Therefore, because of the gendered nature of tourism employment as discussed above, Purcell (1996) poses the question "if women are routinely seen as (indeed, employed as) sex objects, what implications does this have for their career development opportunities, as individuals and as a category?" (p.20).

Muslim women face additional barriers and issues in addition to the low pay and status of tourism work. Because Muslim women are subject to specific religious and culture norms, as discussed earlier, the negative aspects of tourism employment may be particularly problematic and difficult to overcome, especially where tourism employment is mostly dominated by men (Swain, 1995). Due to the social expectation for women to maintain their responsibilities as mothers and primary family caretakers, Muslim women may feel that they are unable to accept full time jobs or be engaged in occupations with non-standard working hours. Also Muslim women's opportunities in the tourism industry may be particularly constrained since they may be less likely to have the necessary skills. This is because employment in the tourism industry is mostly based on qualification as indicated by Hjalager and Andersen (2001).

Islamic cultural beliefs about tourism can also constrain women's employment in this industry. In some ways, Islamic beliefs can be seen to complement travel and tourism for example by encouraging Muslims to help travellers (Aziz, 2001; Henderson, 2003), to host and interact with travellers, to travel to other countries (Din, 1989), and to fulfill religious pilgrimage (Sindiga, 1996). At the same time, there is also conflict between modern western tourism and Islamic cultures with tourism seen to dilute the interpretation of Islamic culture (Burns & Cooper, 1997). For example, the behaviors and dress of tourists, sexual permissiveness, gambling, and consumption of pork and alcohol are seen to be inappropriate and offensive (Ritter, 1975; Henderson, 2003). Because of this, many Muslim societies have taken a cautious view of tourism in order to protect the community and culture from the western influence of in-coming modern tourism (Baum & Conlin, 1997). These issues raise particular difficulties with respect to the employment of Muslim women in the tourism industry. Tourism employment brings women into contact with strangers from other cultures, and this could be considered to be inappropriate, unappealing or strongly objectionable. Thus, as Sonmez (2001) says, Muslim women's opportunities for employment in this industry will continue to be constrained unless attitudes change about the acceptability of this type of work for women. Overall, tourism employment may cause further difficulties for Muslim women pursuing a career in tourism employment.

Despite all the problems associated with tourism jobs, tourism employment can also be seen as being accessible, and accommodating a wide variety of skills. This can be seen as a benefit for those who want to move away from non-tourism employment (Szivas & Riley, 1999). It is an industry that women can join without any formal training, especially since they have experience from their domestic chores as wives and mothers, for example serving meals, working in kitchens, making beds, and so forth. The seasonality of tourism employment may also suit women who have family responsibilities and other duties (Riley, Ladkin & Szivas, 2002).

Apart from accessibility of tourism work, Purcell (1997) suggests that women may actively seek tourism work as it seen as more "fun" than other types of work. Purcell (1997) also suggests that the fact that it is seen as "women's work" may even make it more attractive to some women. In addition, some researchers suggest that the nature of tourism employment, including traveling and meeting people, may be an incentive to women that counteracts some of the negative aspects (Riley et al, 2002). In some ways, therefore, women who seek jobs in the tourism industry could be seen as agents, making deliberate choices about employment, rather than succumbing to gender and employment discrimination (Phillimore, 2002).

Summary

It is clear from the literature review that Muslim women continue to face various religious and cultural constraints such as male domination, dress code strictness, segregation, limited rights, early marriages and family obligations. This, in turn, limits their positioning in terms of their status, rights, education and access to employment. Although Islam has provided certain rights to Muslim women, many of these rights are not honored due to what can be seen as a misinterpretation of Islam and the perspectives of Muslim men. Certain negative stereotypes of Muslim women still persist in the West, where Muslim women are seen as oppressed, weak and submissive. These stereotypes, though, are misleading too, since the lives of individual Muslim women vary and intra-country differences are also evident. Thus, despite the issues affecting Muslim women's status in the Middle East, there is a potential for a change in women's status through employment. Although the Middle East struggles to adapt to globalization and modernization, these changes are promising and are opening up doors for Muslim women.

The review of the literature also revealed that the issue of Muslim women's employment in the Middle East has not been investigated thoroughly to date. While there are some problems related to the accuracy of official statistics on employment patterns for Muslim women, it is evident that female labor force participation is lower in Muslim countries compared to non-Muslim countries. There are several reasons for this, relating back to cultural and religious constraints. Other reasons include the lack of jobs for women, early marriages, child bearing, and lack of childcare and domestic chores. Despite these problems, there has been a growth of female labor force participation rates in the Middle East, associated with better educational opportunities, the availability of government jobs, increased support for employed women and more specifically, the development of certain industries such as tourism. It has been argued that the tourism industry is likely to provide increased employment opportunities for Muslim women. However, it is still unclear as to whether tourism employment will help to overcome the issues and constraints that Muslim women face when it comes to their status in their society.

Besides religious and cultural constraints, the literature has showed that there are many problems surrounding tourism employment for women. These include the gendered nature of tourism employment and unstable, low status and poorly paid types of jobs that are available for women. Thus employment in the tourism industry can be seen to be exploitative. On the other hand, women may also benefit from tourism employment if this form of work is seen to be accessible, flexible, fun, and appropriate for women.

Clearly, then, there are both advantages and disadvantages when it comes to tourism employment for Muslim women. Such employment may have the potential to lead to increased status, independence, and empowerment for Muslim women, but there may also be a downside in terms of exploitative work, the burden of work and family obligation, and religious and cultural constraints. This, then, raises the question of how tourism employment affects women and women's lives. Does it lead to greater empowerment and independence or does it lead to exploitation and a heavy burden due to combining paid work and family work? Also, more generally, does female employment in the tourism industry challenge or reinforce traditional, constructing views of women and femininity?

This analysis of the literature reveals the need for better understanding of the issues surrounding tourism employment for Muslim women. Accordingly, this study explores the perspectives and experiences of Muslim women employed in the tourism industry. The study adopts a gender relation's perspective, focusing on women, the gendered nature of their employment, and the employment-related constraints that they face. The study also addresses the positive aspects of this type of employment for women, including its potential for women's empowerment.

It is important to pursue this research in Muslim societies in order to have a better understanding of Islamic cultures and cultural differences. This in turn may help increase information about the roles that Muslim women play in the modern world and help reduce many of the negative stereotypes held about Muslim women. The need to understand such issues surrounding women was emphasized by Liu and

Wall (2006), who suggested that one of the topics that requires further research is the involvement of women in the tourism industry and the difficulties and challenges that they face as employees. Moreover, research is required related to the cultural implications of tourism employment for women (Sinclair, 1997), including whether tourism can help to improve women's situation or whether it reinforces constraints and stereotypes. The methodological process used in this research study will be discussed in detail in the following chapter.

Chapter 3: The Research Process

The purpose of the research process chapter is to explain the approach and methods that were adopted in conducting the research on Muslim women employed in the tourism industry. As the aim of this study is to understand the experiences and meanings of tourism employment for Muslim women in the Middle East, an interpretive approach using grounded theory and qualitative interviews was used to gather Muslim women's perspectives towards this form of employment. As mentioned earlier, although the Middle East shares certain commonalities in terms of religion and cultural ideologies towards women, women's experiences are diversified due to varying socio-economic, political and cultural arrangements in different Middle Eastern countries. Thus, the study was conducted in Oman, as the research site and cultural setting for this study. Based on the purpose of the research and the review of related literature, the study explored the experiences of Muslim women who were working in the tourism industry in Oman. In particular, the study examined the women's meanings of tourism work, the benefits and challenges of working in the tourism industry for these women, and their perspectives on the importance of tourism work for Muslim women in Oman.

This chapter will first present information about the research site in terms of the tourism industry in Oman, and the status, employment situation, and various constraints affecting Muslim women in that country. This provides a background to the research setting and the process that was employed. An explanation of the theoretical paradigm that guided this study will be provided and how it applies to this particular study. Furthermore, a description of the grounded theory methodology that was adopted will be discussed. A description of the recruitment and selection is then provided, followed by the background information about the women. The collection process that was undertaken is described in detail, as well as information about the steps that were taken in analyzing the data and how the analysis helped to answer the research questions. Lastly, issues associated with member checks and with ethics are also discussed. In sum, the goal of the research process chapter is to provide an understanding of the processes and steps that were taken in conducting the research in order to address the research questions.

The Research Site

The geographical location of Oman has been described by Choufany and Younes (2005) as being "located on the southern tip of the Arabia Peninsula and is bordered by the Arabian Sea to the east. The country has land borders with the United Arab Emirates, Saudi Arabia and Yemen" (p. 2). The capital of Oman is Muscat, which has a population of over 600,000 and is described as "the commercial heart of the country" (Choufany & Younes, 2005, p. 3). The emergence of Oman as a tourist destination began only in the mid 1990s, so tourism in Oman is seen as a new phenomenon (Mershen, 2007). The country's earlier economic development had come mainly from the production and export of oil (Inskeep, 1994). But due to the need to diversify their economy, the government looked to tourism as an area for future economic growth and a major source of foreign exchange.

The Oman government approached tourism carefully by adopting a policy to encourage quality tourism. Its main objective was to maximize the potential economic benefits of tourism within some limitations, based on the desire to protect cultural values and the environment (Sadek, 2000). Accordingly, the country's tourism development focus was based on promoting its natural, cultural and historic features rather than creating a mass tourism market (Inskeep, 1994). The first directorate of tourism was established under the Ministry of Commerce and Industry in 2002 and the Ministry of Tourism was then established in mid 2004 (Choufany & Younes, 2005). The development of the tourism industry in Oman was focused on building prestigious five star hotel projects such as the Al-Bustan Palace hotel, the Intercontinental, Crown Plaza, and others (Mershen, 2007). In 2003, the total number of hotels in Oman was 133 and the total number of hotel-beds was 9,778 (Oman Ministry of National Economy as cited in Winckler, 2007).

Besides the offering of luxury hotels as an attractive characteristic of the Oman tourism industry, Oman offers unmatched natural, cultural and heritage resources (Abdul-Ghani, 2006). Specifically, the country has a wide and diverse landscape, which includes coastal, beaches, desert and mountain (Winckler, 2007). According to Ain al-Yaqeen, "Oman offers some of the cleanest, most stunning beaches a visitor could hope to see" (as cited in Winckler, 2007, p. 226). In addition, the country possesses unique local traditional manufacturing and heritage, which is offered by the indigenous society of Oman, the Bedouins (Winckler, 2007). Thus, Oman could be seen a unique destination in offering distinctive tourism characteristics. In terms of purpose of visits, Oman has been primarily characterized by leisure visitation. Specifically, about 52% of rooms in 2004 were generated from leisure demand and 39% by business demand (Government of Oman as cited in Choufany & Younes, 2005). Since Oman's tourism industry is promoted by offering high tourism quality, the focus has been on attracting "high end" tourists (Winckler, 2007). As for tourists region of origin, tourists from Middle East countries accounted for 53% of the room nights in Muscat in 2003. Europeans accounted for 18% and Asians for 16% in the same year (Government of Oman as cited in Choufany & Younes, 2005).

As part of the national tourism plan for Oman that was prepared in 1991 by the UNDP (United Nations Development Program) and the WTO (World Tourism Organization), attention was paid to the issue of "manpower" planning (Inskeep, 1994). This was deemed important because the image of the hotel and catering industry as a source of employment was poor, due to cultural, religious and social concerns. Traditionally, tourism had not been viewed as a possible employment area in Oman. There were also difficulties associated with attracting local people to work in the private sector due to the attractiveness of working in the public sector. However, the government implemented a policy to increase local population participation in the workforce, including tourism. Another manpower planning issue was that Omani women traditionally did not work outside their homes (Inskeep, 1994). According to the AHDR report (as cited in Alvi, 2005), Oman had the lowest female percentage employment in the Middle East at 8.6% in 1997. However, this seems to be changing rapidly. Although there is a lack of official statistics displaying current rates of employment, female national employment in Oman is now officially encouraged by the authorities (Mansfeld & Winckler, 2008).

The initial tourism plan in Oman included the need to attract women to tourism employment because Omani female employees had a reputation for high productivity and punctuality. The plan also addressed challenges that the country faced because of the traditional reluctance of the local population to work in tourism or to consider tourism as a desirable career (Inskeep, 1994). The plan was successful in that many new jobs in tourism were taken by Omani nationals and included a sizable proportion of women employees (Winckler, 2007). With protected growth of the tourism industry in Oman, Kapur (2005) estimated that about 115,000 jobs in the tourism industry would be generated by 2014. Omani nationals can be found working in various tourism sectors, which include hotel, catering, airline and tour guide jobs.

The issue of employment through tourism received even greater attention during the mid 1990s when the Omani authorities realized that the tourism industry had more potential compared to other non-oil industries and had the potential to contribute to the national long-term socio-economic development plan. A second plan entitled 'The vision for Oman's economy: Oman 2020', was developed by the Omani authorities and included three main goals; diversification, privatization and Omanization. One of the main targets of the Omani authorities through development of their tourism industry was to generate massive additional employment opportunities for both high and low skilled personnel. The other main target of the authorities was to increase female labor force participation rates. In the early 1990s, the importance of increasing the national labor force participation rates was related to the desire to "achieve reduction of the huge dependency ratio (resulting from the low labor force participation rates) and simultaneously to bring about fertility decline" (Winckler, 2007, p.225). Furthermore, the authorities wanted to contribute to the promotion of female employment in the tourism field. Although Oman is officially a Muslim country, it has a moderate approach to religion, and alcohol is legal in certain circumstances. Newspaper articles had reported that Omani nationals were open to accepting jobs at modest salaries (Gulf News letter as cited in Winckler, 2007). Thus, the development of the tourism industry was seen to provide new work opportunities for nationals, and especially female nationals, who might be more willing to accept lower salaries.

However, despite the enthusiasm of members of the tourism industry in Oman, a delay in the tourism development plan took place. This appears to have been due to the authorities' fear of the socio-political consequences of rapid change brought about by mass international tourism. For example, a senior officer in the Ministry of Commerce and Industry was quoted as saying, "we feel it is important for us to maintain our identity and culture and we know from experience that thousands of tourists pouring into a specific area can drastically alter the delicate visitor/host balance" (Arnold, p.20, 2007).

The emergence of the tourism industry in Oman took place sometime later, when the traditional Omani attitude towards tourism began to change, primarily due to economic difficulties, low oil revenues, and awareness of income and employment opportunities through tourism. Structural unemployment was a major problem for the Omani economy during the early 1990s, despite the rapid socio-economic progress that had taken place during the 1970s and 1980s. By the 1990s, the labor market consisted of only two markets. One was for nationals employed exclusively by the public sector, with high salaries and good working conditions. The other market comprised the private sector, which employed exclusively foreign labor at low salaries. The traditional idea of working for the public sector was favored by young Omani graduates. For example, Lancaster quotes a young Omani entrepreneur in the tourism industry who said, "if you find a governmental-paid position you are set for life" (p.33 as cited in Winckler, 2007, p.224). This attitude continued, and the total number of Omani nationals in the private sector represented less than 15% of the total private sector workforce with the rest being comprised of foreign workers as of June 2002 (Winckler, 2007).

In terms of women' status, one of the main political and social objectives of Sultan Qaboos, the ruler of Oman since the 1970s, was to organize new constituencies for groups that were disadvantaged, including women. Oman is perceived to be one of the most progressive monarchies of the Arabian Peninsula in terms of introducing women into the national development plan. However, it has been noted that women in Oman still face various social, economic and political barriers. Women's roles and status are structurally determined by state ideology, and also by the level and type of economic development and by class location (Riphenburg, 1998). Moreover, the position of women in Oman has been restricted by the country's semi-peripheral position in the world economic system; it's high reliance on oil revenues and its limited resources. The Sultan, though, wanted to reduce the disadvantages that women faced and promote their entry into the labor market. Thus, women's employment patterns were primarily influenced by the political economy of Oman (Riphenburg, 1998).

Government jobs in Oman are generally thought to be more acceptable for women compared to private sector employment. This is because women employed in the public sector are less likely to be "on view" in the public, and because government jobs provide equal pay for men and women. Also, government-employed women receive good maternity leave benefits, which include two months of paid leave and one to two years of unpaid leave. In the late 1990s, it was estimated that women made up about 13% of Oman's governmental employees and that they were usually found in traditional female fields. However, these positions were mostly filled by women from elite and middle class families, as well as by women who were educated abroad, suggesting the influence of class, income and education on job opportunities for women (Riphenburg, 1998).

Social attitudes are more conservative towards women employed in the private sector, and women hold few administrative and managerial occupations in this sector. Nevertheless, women are found at many levels of private sector employment, such as employment as bank officials, hotel managers, entrepreneurs, secretaries, and so forth. Women with higher education can also obtain higher salaries and more fulfilling careers in this sector. Riphenburg (1998) has described Omani women as working out of a sense of duty to their country or out of desire for self-fulfillment. Also, childcare may not necessarily be a major barrier to women due to the availability of domestic help, including family and paid help. However, financial constraints may force women to work and to reduce the number of children they have (Riphenburg, 1998).

In terms of marriage, there is a high value placed on the institution of marriage in Oman as in other Muslim societies. Although Omani women have the choice to work, the idea of employment as an alternative to marriage may not be seen as a viable solution. Traditionally, Omani women married in their late teens, but age at marriage is now often delayed for several years due to the spread of education. Women have also traditionally gained status when they produced children, especially sons. Similarly to women in some other Muslim countries, the lives of Omani women remain under the control of their husbands, fathers and brothers. Thus, Riphenburg (1998) concluded, "women in Oman remain an underutilized human resource because of limited industrialization and traditional definition of women's role" (p.151). Nevertheless, Omani women do traditionally have some power in terms of influencing family decision-making. Since the traditional Oman society is comprised of kinship relationships based on social and economic ties within their family (Riphenbrug, 1998), this suggests that women may use their power in family decision making to make female employment more acceptable. Thus, with the development of the tourism industry and its potential growth, some women in Oman are benefitting from tourism employment.

Overall, Oman provided an appropriate opportunity for understanding the experiences of Muslim women employed in the tourism industry. This is because Oman is a Muslim country with many of the traditional Muslims values that are shared with other countries in the Middle East. Also, the status of women in Oman is similar to that of other Muslim societies in the Middle East. More importantly, Oman is a country in which tourism is being promoted, and women workers are needed to fill tourism jobs. Thus, Oman was determined to be a useful site to examine women's experiences of work in the tourism industry, to explore how they feel about their jobs, their work and family responsibilities, and to gain an understanding of the implications of female employment for women's status in this particular Muslim society.

Theoretical Paradigm

The paradigm that guided my study was social constructionism, which according to Daly (2007), "is rooted in a belief that all reality is a constructed reality" (p.31). That is, the assumption is that women's experiences are socially constructed, and the way women experience their everyday working experiences will be a result of their knowledge of the world and how their sense of self is constructed (Small, 1999). Creswell (2003) describes the assumptions that are held about social constructionism as,

> Individuals seek understanding of the world in which they live and work. They develop subjective meanings of their experiences-meanings directed towards certain objects or things. These meanings are varied and multiple, leading the researcher to look for the complexity of views rather than narrowing meanings into a few categories or ideas (p.8).

This paradigm was adopted to help develop an understanding of how women tourism employees experience and make sense of their everyday life situations, and how this relates to the socio-cultural environment in which they live. The paradigm was seen to help in the exploration of both positive and negative experiences and meanings of women's tourism employment, and the influence of cultural attitudes towards women and women's employment. At the same time, the paradigm suggests that societal attitudes are also socially constructed, thus sensitizing me to the possibility that tourism employment might also influence broader societal perspectives.

Social constructionism is based on several elements including ontology (the nature of reality); epistemology (how the world is known, the relationship between the enquirer and the known); and methodology (how knowledge is gained about the world) (Small, 1999). In regards to the ontology, constructionism assumes that the nature of reality is based on a social culture that is created by humans. This social culture forms the everyday living situation that we encounter. With regards to epistemology, social constructionism has both a subjective and an objective stance. As Daly (2007) points out, within the social constructionism paradigm, the researcher "accepts the presence of an external reality that is subjectively perceived and understood from the perspective of the observer" (p.32). And lastly, in terms of methodology, the grounded theory methodology is consistent with the social constructionism paradigm, because it helped to present and conceptualize the lived experiences of the women. Small (1999) has emphasized that when choosing a method for research with women, it is important to allow women to express their thoughts and feelings in their own words rather than to respond to the words of the researcher. This was further emphasized by Reinharz (1992) when she said that "this asset is particularly important for the study of women because in this way learning from women is an antidote to centuries of ignoring women's ideas altogether or having men speak for women" (p.19). This further supports the use of a grounded theory methodology for analyzing the experiences and meanings of tourism employment through capturing the voices of the women.

Using Grounded Theory

A constructivist grounded theory approach was used for this study to enhance theoretical understanding of modern women's employment in the tourism field (Charmaz, 2006). According to Charmaz (2006), "a constructivist approach places priority on the phenomena of study and sees both data and analysis as created from shared experiences and relationships with participants" (p. 130). This approach allowed me to play an active role in organizing and assigning categories to the data in order to construct the central underlying meaning of the women's experiences. Furthermore, constructivist grounded theory allowed me to approach the research issue with theoretical sensitivity based on prior experiences, concepts, ideas and theory. As mentioned earlier, I am from Oman and I am familiar with the Omani cultural, Islamic teachings and tourism employment. This background and personal experience assisted me in conducting the interviews with the women. Further, special attention to the interpretive process, allowed me to construct the themes and sub-themes in a meaningful way. Thus, I believe an "intimate familiarity" was accomplished through my involvement, and understanding (Blumer, 1969) and through being a woman and looking at women's experiences.

Grounded theory allowed me to be flexible and creative in collecting and interpreting the data in order to understand the meanings of Muslim women's experiences in tourism employment. According to Charmaz (2006), a grounded theory approach allows the researcher to see the data in fresh ways and to explore ideas about the data collected by using early analytic writing. This assisted me to construct an original analysis of the data collected by making memos during the early stages of the data collection and analysis.

I believe that the grounded theory approach is consistent with my own beliefs, values and assumptions. As Charmaz (2006) explains, "we are part of the world we study and the data we collect. We construct our grounded theories through our past and present involvement and interactions with people, perspectives and research practices"(p.10). I also believe that I played a very personal role in the research due to the fact that I am a Muslim woman myself. Daly (2007) says that "researchers play a powerful role in shaping how these realities are brought forward by participants" (p. 33). Through the social constructionism paradigm, I explored women's views of tourism employment and I took precautions in being aware of and acknowledging how my interpretations developed from my own personal, cultural and historical experiences (Charmaz, 2006). This was achieved by making notes of ideas and thoughts in a personal reflective journal. Through this process, I aimed to develop new theoretical understandings of women's employment in the tourism field.

Although the purpose was not to create a fully developed grounded theory, thematic analysis facilitated an understanding of the meanings and experiences of Muslim women employed in the tourism industry. Hence, this approach allowed me to better understand the role of tourism employment in the lives of Muslim women.

Recruitment and Participants

The women that were interviewed for this qualitative study were selected through the use of convenience sampling. Veal (2006) describes convenience sampling as a technique, which conveniently uses located persons or organizations (e.g., friends, colleagues, etc.). This technique was appropriate for this study since I already had established networks with women working in the Oman tourism industry. Thus, I began the data collection phase by contacting women I knew working in the tourism industry through telephone calls or face-to-face meetings. During these initial meetings or telephone calls, I explained to them about my study and asked if they would be willing to participate. While recruiting the women for the interviews, I tried to get a range of single, married and married with children participants in order to provide different perspectives and experiences. After agreeing on the time, date and place for the interview, I would provide each participant with the information letter about my study either in person or by email.

From the initial interviews that I conducted, a snowball technique was then used as a means to meet further women. According to Patton (1980), the snowball technique is described as an approach where participants are asked to suggest other people who might participate in the study. Thus, I would ask the women that I interviewed to suggest other women, who would be possible participants for the interviews. Many of the women did refer me to other women, and they would contact these women first for the referral and I would then make a follow up contact to set up an interview with them. This procedure turned out to be very successful. Although I did have some difficulty with setting up interviews with some women, I successfully conducted 9 interviews with local Muslim women working in the Oman tourism industry (out of a total of 18 women contacted). Thus, I was able to achieve the initial target sample of interviewing 5-10 women.

Information About The Women

The following is some summary information about the women that I interviewed, including background information about age, martial status, education level, history of employment and current employment. The women's names are not identified in order to protect their identity and privacy, and pseudonyms names were assigned instead.

- Fatima is a single woman in her late 20's. She holds a high school certificate and an IATA (International Airline Transport Association) certificate. She worked in the tourism industry for nine years, and this included working as a tour consultant and at various hotel positions. Fatima currently works full time as a guest relation's manager in a large hotel.
- Aisha is a single woman in her mid 20's. She holds a master's degree in tourism management. She has worked in the tourism industry for two years, which included working as an events co-coordinator in an incentive tour company and front desk staff member at a large hotel. She currently works full time as a sales and marketing co-coordinator at a large hotel.
- Laila is a single woman in her mid 20's. She holds a bachelors degree in hotel management and tourism. She worked in the tourism industry for about three years in various hotel positions in different large hotels. She currently works full time as a front desk supervisor at a small hotel.
- Khadija is a single woman in her mid 20's. She holds a diploma in tourism and hospitality management. She worked in the tourism industry for about three years as an event coordinator. She currently works full time as a customer service representative at a tourism resort.
- Salwa is a single woman in her late 20's. She holds a marketing diploma. She worked in the tourism industry for about five years in sales for two large hotels. She currently works full time as an assistant director for sales and marketing in a large hotel.
- Shariffa is a married woman in her early 30's with two children, aged five and two. She holds a national vocational certificate in travel and tourism. She worked in the tourism industry for about 9 years in a travel agency and an airline. She is currently searching for a different job due to the recent closure of the airline company.
- Zuewna is a married woman in her late 30's, with two children. She holds a bachelors degree in hotel management. She worked in the tourism industry for about nine years in a large hotel. She currently runs her own full-time business.
- Nadia is a married woman in her early 30's with two children, aged 2 and 1. She holds a diploma in hospitality management. She worked in the tourism industry for about nine years in various hotel

positions in a large hotel. She currently works full time as an office manager at a tourism development company and is studying part time for a bachelor's degree in hotel management.
- Munira is a married woman in her mid 20's, with no children. She holds a high school diploma. She worked in the tourism industry for about four years in a travel agency and a large hotel. She currently works full time as a front desk staff member at a large hotel and is studying part time for a marketing management degree.

Data Collection

The data were collected through open-ended interviews conducted face to face in English, since all participants were comfortable with the English language. A semi structured interview format, which as outlined by Finn, Elliott-White and Walton (2000), has the advantage that it "combines the flexibility of the unstructured interview with comparability of key questions" (p.74). It also allows probing in order to seek clarification and elaboration when a particular idea or concept emerges during the interviews (Finn et al, 2000). On the other hand, Finn et al. (2000) explain that the disadvantage of this type of interview is that "bias may increase as the interviewer selects questions to probe and may inhibit comparability of responses" (p.74). Therefore, as far as possible, I sought to raise the same issues with all the women, and in a similar way, while also being open to new ideas and topics, and encouraging the women to talk about their experiences and perspectives of tourism employment.

I believe that interviews were an appropriate qualitative method for my study, based on Jennings (2005) description that " interviews are used to make sense of and understand on a daily basis the world in which we live, at either the informal or formal level" (p. 99). Thus, it was through the interviews that I was able to gain a better understanding of the Muslim women's meanings and experiences in tourism employment by allowing the women to express their perceptions of reality. Although Jennings (2005) cautions that interviews are mostly associated with the western world, she does emphasize "interviewing is becoming a global research method for understanding and making sense of the lives of the peoples of this world" (p.99). This is due to globalization, internationalization, spread of the knowledge economy and western research practices. Therefore, conducting the interviews in Oman was successful despite the fact that this type of interview is new in Oman. The women that I interviewed were very happy to participate in my study and shared their experiences quite openly. I would often be asked about the topic of the study, which they all found amusing because no such research had been conducted in Oman before. They thought it was important to conduct research in such areas.

Jennings (2005) describes the interview as "a social interaction/interchange. It is a two-way exchange. Knowledge, understanding and learning are at the roots of qualitative interview engagements" (p. 102). This is consistent, too, with the social constructionism approach and grounded theory (Charmaz, 2006). Jennings (2005) also cautions that qualitative interviews may appear to be easy. She explains that "the very nature, diversity and complexity amongst qualitative interview forms and the resulting complex, dynamic and indeterminate nature of social interaction inherent in such interviews become problematic in attempting to capture that which is socially constructed and contextualized as well as historically situated in time" (p.103). Despite knowing three of the participants, I still needed to establish rapport with the women in order to ensure the success of the interviews. Also knowing three of the participants did not appear to influence the interviews. Both the participants I knew, and the ones I had not met before, appeared to be open and comfortable discussing their experiences. The interviews that I conducted were semi formal, where humor and free expression were used in the conversation. Thus, I was able to develop social relationship, trust and respect with the women (Jennings, 2005).

Since the study was based on a grounded theory approach, the number of interviews was guided by theoretical sampling. According to Jennings (2005), "theoretical sampling guides material collection and analysis and contributes to the determination of when to stop sampling" (p.111). In the final interviews, I sensed the collected interviews were sufficient for the analysis and I decided to stop sampling because I was getting similar responses with the women.

The interviews were conducted in Oman from October to November 2008. I had chosen this time frame because this is the high tourism season in Oman and it is the time when most participants were likely to be available. This decision was made based on my awareness of the customs and operations of the working environment in Oman. The interviews with the women lasted approximately from 1 to 1 ½ hours, and varied to some extent with the level of engagement that I had with the women. In order to ensure convenience for the women, the interviews were conducted at various locations, either in their homes, coffee shops, or work places.

In collecting the data, an interview guide was used. Although I have limited experience in conducting qualitative interviews, the interview guide gave me the confidence to carry out the interviews successfully. The questions used in the interview guide were general, broad and open-ended in order to cover all relevant topics during the interviews. Basic background information about the women was collected at the beginning of the interviews, such as marital status, number and ages of children, educational background and work experience. This provided an overall picture of each woman's life. Following this introductory part of the interview, specific issues and topics were than raised for discussion. These included questions related to the benefits of tourism employment, religious and cultural constraints, and the implications of tourism employment for the empowerment and status of women. For example, questions related to the benefits of tourism employment included the types of benefits received from their workplace. As for religious and cultural constraints, these questions focused on the difficulties and challenges encountered at work, and the attitudes of family members toward employment in the tourism industry. All of the women (single, married without children and married with children) were asked about the various constraints that they faced related to work and home-based responsibilities, but the specific issues discussed varied according to martial and other factors. Lastly, empowerment and status issues were addressed by asking the women whether or not they thought that tourism employment could and does help provide Muslim women with power, status and independence.

After receiving the women's consent, the interviews were all recorded and later transcribed. Tape-recording the interviews was beneficial, as Patton says that, "a good tape recorder enables the social interaction to be recorded authentically" (as cited in Jennings, 2005 p. 111). Furthermore, Silverman says that, "transcripts of audio-recording provide superior accounts of the natural interaction within an interview" (as cited in Jennings, 2005 p.111). And lastly, although transcribing interviews took considerable time, the transcripts allowed for a thorough analysis of all of the data.

A reflective research journal was maintained in keeping track of my memos, thoughts, feelings, observations and questions about the process and each interview session. Reflecting on my own thoughts was important because of my background as an Omani Muslim and my passion for the field of tourism. Also through the journal, I recorded analytic notes during the analysis process.

Data Analysis

While the findings of the study are not generalizable, and this was not the purpose of the study, information from women in different life situations (e.g. single, married, etc.) was collected. Thus, some comparisons between single and married women were made. At the same time, a "working picture of the broader social structure" was developed, as advocated by Henderson (1991, p.132), to provide an overall picture on tourism employment for these Omani women.

The analysis process that was undertaken was adopted from Charmaz (2006). During the analysis process, I used hard copies of the transcripts as well as Microsoft word to help organize my analysis at each step. The analysis process was broken down into three stages of grounded theory coding (i.e., initial coding, focused coding, and theoretical coding) with each stage involving several steps.

Initial coding.

This process involved naming the data by using line-by-line coding (Charmaz, 2006). I decided to use line-by-line coding as it allowed me to have a good understanding of the data as well as to avoid excluding any valuable information. First, I conducted line-by-line coding, where I used hard copies of the interview transcripts. I attempted to give a code for each line and I used a highlighter to select the words in the sentence that made up the code, either with new codes or with existing code names as appropriate. After coding all of the interviews, I then transferred my initial codes from the hard copies to a word document in a table format with women 1, 2, etc. This allowed me to see the codes clearly, and also to remove some redundant codes. During this process, I was able to sense the commonalities within the interviews as many of the codes that I developed appeared across all the interviews.

Focused coding.

Focused coding involved identifying the codes that best captured the women's expressed meanings and that were deemed to be the most helpful in terms of the formation of possible categories. This process also involved comparing data both within and across the interviews in terms of how they related to the developed categories (Charmaz, 2006). While I was conducting line-by-line coding, I was already getting a sense of the types of categories that were emerging from the interviews by identifying common and variable patterns in the data. Therefore, in order to categorize my codes, I developed some initial common categories (e.g., work difficulties, women in tourism, tourism benefits, personal gains, family attitudes towards tourism, husbands' attitudes towards tourism, etc.). I then went through a hard copy of my coding table and highlighted each code according to the categories it fell under. Subsequently, I transferred those codes from the table into a regular word document, where the codes were assigned to each of the categories I had developed. I then needed to narrow down or focus and define the codes for each of these categories. This was done by looking at the commonalities of the codes for each interview that fell under each category. This led to the development of initial themes that included data and categories with similar meanings, and helped to enhance understanding of the interview data as a whole. These initial themes were then carefully inspected and examined to determine the properties that best defined the meanings and concepts that formed each theme.

Theoretical coding.

This final stage of coding involved the process of theorizing about categories by examining relationships between the themes, which had been developed during the focused coding stage. The overall purpose of this stage was to explain how all the themes worked together in the overall process (Charmaz, 2006). I was already able to sense the emerging themes and the relationships between the themes, as there was considerable commonality among the women in terms of their experiences in tourism employment. At the final stages of the analysis, I compared my emerging themes and properties with the literature in order to relate my findings with existing ideas, concepts, and theories to determine commonalities and discrepancies. Overall, the above analysis process helped to answer the specific research questions based on the themes, properties, and relationships among the themes.

I believe that through this process and the development of themes and relationships among themes, I was able to give voice to the women whose voices might have been marginalized in large-scale quantitative studies (Jordan & Gibson, 2004). By looking at emerging themes from the data and comparing and constructing, I explored the various issues of tourism employment for Muslim women. I also revisited the literature review and drew on existing theories and literature as the analysis progressed (Jordan & Gibson, 2004). Furthermore, I also revisited my reflective notes that I made while conducting the interviews and analyzing the data in order to compare my notes with the emerging themes. As Strauss and Corbin emphasize, "researchers are not without knowledge and the theoretical sensitivity of the researcher is useful in that it plays a role in identifying and interpreting the patterns within the data" (as cited in Jordan & Gibson, 2004, p.227). In other words, I used my own insight and understanding in developing the themes.

Validation and Presentation of Findings

In order to help strengthen the credibility of the findings, a member check was conducted during the final stages of the study (Creswell, 2003). All of the women were interested in receiving information about the study findings, so a feedback letter and a summary of the study results was emailed to each of the women for feedback. From the 9 women that I interviewed, 4 of the women provided brief feedback, which in all cases was supportive of and helped to confirm my summary of the study results.

Ethical Issues

During the recruitment and selection process, an information letter was provided to potential participants, so that they were fully informed about the research purposes, process, and of their options. A signed informed consent form was also collected from each of the women prior to each interview. The women were informed of their right to decline to answer any questions and that they were free to withdraw from the interview process and from the study at anytime.

Throughout the research process, I was aware of possible issues that may come up. One of the specific ethical challenges that I was aware of was confidentiality. Although there were no issues with their families, colleagues and bosses with the women's involvement in the study, confidentiality was still guaranteed to the women, who were informed that their interview data would be kept secure. I am not sure whether families, colleagues and bosses were informed about or aware of the women's involvement in the interviews. To take extra precautions on this, I informed the women, before proceeding with the interview taping, not to mention people's names or company names. I also informed the women that their names would not be used in the study, but that pseudonyms would be used.

Another possible ethical challenge was the discussion of delicate and difficult issues, such as family and martial relationships, perspectives on gender/gender roles/exploitation of women, and discussions of religion, religious and other constraints. Although these may have been more sensitive than other issues, the women seemed to be comfortable and willing to discuss all of these topics. Before starting the interviews, I asked the women if they had any questions about the study or their participation. By signing the consent form, as mentioned above, the women were informed of the formal ethics review process that my research went through. I felt that since I am a woman, a wife, a mother and an Omani, this made the women comfortable discussing such issues, and I felt that they were able to relate to me. Furthermore, as many of the interviews were set up through referrals, as discussed earlier, this may also have made the women more comfortable and secure. In addition, the interview questions were constructed carefully, so as to give each woman the option of whether or not to respond, and how to respond. Nevertheless, none of the women seemed to be uncomfortable, and none declined to answer any of the questions.

Chapter 4: Findings

The analysis process led to the development of seven themes. The themes illustrate the commonalities of experiences and meanings that were shared by the women as well as the various factors that may have influenced these experiences. The seven main themes relate to finding work in the tourism field, facing negative attitudes, challenges of tourism work, dealing with negative attitudes and challenges, importance of tourism work in the women lives, an expanded vision of tourism work, and implications for social change.

Theme 1: Finding Work in the Tourism Field

The first theme sets the stage, and details the various influences and expectations that women face in searching for work in general. This leads to information about and explanation of how they found work in the tourism industry.

1.1 Choosing tourism as a career choice.

When asked about their entry into the work force after completing high school, many of the women talked about giving tourism employment a chance as a career choice. At the beginning, the women typically did not have a strong notion of the types of career they wanted, but they felt the need to have a job. For example, Fatima stated,

> Ok, when I started, it was basically, it was a job, I needed a job, you know, I wasn't going to study abroad, I wasn't... you know, I had to get a job because my dad always taught me that independence is important and I needed to start paying my way, so that's how I started, I started as it's just a job, I didn't think about it as the tourism or the hotel industry is... I didn't know anything.

Salwa described tourism employment as being a pure coincidence:

> My initial, actually, initial idea was to do pharmacy but because that didn't work out, plan B was to do my degree. And it was available [undergraduate education] and everybody was doing it, so I thought "ok" but once that was done, I didn't really have a clue of where I was going. So me landing into the hotel industry was pure coincidence.

Some of the women did have family encouragement, with family members suggesting that they give tourism a try. For example, Zuewna said, "my aunt was working at the hotel industry and she suggested, "You have good communications and social skills, why don't you try it out". Nadia was also encouraged by her father to try tourism employment,

I started looking for a job, and then there was, there was a big ad in the newspapers. And because my dad knew somebody in the hotel, he said, 'why don't you try working there?' Ahh, before, I didn't know anything about hotels; I was like "I'll try and see how it goes".

Other women found work in tourism employment through the availability of new tourism education opportunities in Oman, which they found enjoyable. For example, "I wanted to study communications but it wasn't available here in Oman, and ahmm they just opened the tourism and hospitality academy, so my father suggested that I try out and see if I liked it, I did and I loved it" (Aisha). And Khadija said, "so when I got the opportunity to study it (tourism and hospitality education), I was really glad and was happy to study it, I am happy with my choice".

The women were mostly uncertain of tourism employment as a career at the beginning. For Nadia, it was initially intimidating and she felt scared of tourism employment and the requirement of dealing with guests, "I was so scared you know (laughing), very scared [of tourism employment], but than after I was able to deal [confidently] with customer complaints and all that, it was fine but in the beginning it was very scary".

However, the women did see tourism as a new and good opportunity for women. As Shariffa said,

Yeah, the high school, they told me about this. They wanted, you know, to push the Omanis, the local people, to go into the travel industry because there were a lot of us started working. It was maybe only 5% local, so it was different and from the rules of the ministry. In that year, they were focusing more on local [hiring local workers] than anyone, so it was a chance for us, you know, to get into this industry.

This was further emphasized by Khadija as tourism was seen as a new opportunity in Oman, "[it was] very interesting, it was something new and it's just developing in Oman. So it was really a new field, I never thought of something like that".

1.2 Dealing with job access difficulties.

As revealed in the previous section, the women's chance of a tourism career was due to chance, opportunities and encouragement. While searching for jobs at the beginning, the women often encountered difficulties with accessing jobs in general. As Khadija explained, "when I just finished studying, it took me almost 8 month to [find a job], I tried applying at a lot of places and it was really hard to get a job, a whole lot of interviews". Because of these difficulties, many of the women had considered a range of different jobs such as banking, administration and other jobs at the beginning of their career search, "Yes, (laughing) I mean I have applied for jobs in banks, telecommunications, yeah" (Aisha).

One way to gain access to employment was through personal connections, such as family members and friends. As Fatima said, "Ahh, the family connection helped me with getting the first interview. That was the critical one because that was the one where they decide if you go to the next level or not". A similar situation occurred with Laila, who used a family friend to help her get a job,

> Yes, hmmm, I used a family friend. He spoke to them (the hotel). He didn't push it much, but the hotel I worked at needed staff urgently, so it (the personal connection) also helped. And I had to settle for anything, just for experience because a lot of them disregard your internship as an experience.

The women also expressed the importance of having experience, as education alone was not sufficient to secure a job. As a result, many of the women started tourism employment from scratch and built their experience through different jobs and promotions, as explained by Munira,

> The first time I was in the travel agency, so the hotel, they liked to take, at that time, they liked to take [employees] based on having already worked in the hotel industry, already had an experience. They didn't want to take someone and start training from the beginning.

This was further emphasized by Nadia who said, "you need to have [experience], in hotels generally, you need to have experience. They just can't use that [education], you can't just work, you need an experience".

Many of the job search difficulties were associated with the general high job competition in Oman as well being a woman, and the preference for male employees. This meant that the women needed to prove themselves to be the ideal candidate for the particular job to which they were applying. Fatima described her experience of being the only female in a tourism company, "No, it was not easy, it was really hard, hmmm, especially being a women. I will never forget like, I don't know, like in the tourism industry, that tourism company that I worked in". Salwa explained that the increase of job competition in Oman was due to the increase in Omanis obtaining higher education in general:

> But you know, ok, if I look at it from an overall perspective. I would say it's competition, the competition is very hard, you have a lot of people graduating from colleges, universities, hmm you know, with degrees and everything, and they are just trying to grab, grab whatever is available.

1.3 Needing particular skills, personalities and attitudes.

In addition, there was a perception that applicants needed certain skills, personalities and attitudes to gain employment in the tourism industry. In terms of skills, speaking good English played a major role in securing a position in tourism employment. As explained by Fatima, "Britain [English] speaking and that was the main thing that they wanted and they were looking for in Omanis". Having good communications skills, being able to deal with different customers and providing good customer service were also important skills needed to work in tourism employment. Khadija explained the importance of communications when it came to providing good customer service as well as communicating with her peers in the hotel:

> When I started, hmm, mostly like communication... sometimes, communication would be a big issue. It [communication] plays a big role in the hotel and tourism industry in general because it's all about satisfying customers. And you are passing information to a department or passing information from you to the manager or it's all about team work [internal communications], working together, so I thought communication was a very strong skill [for working] in the hotel.

As for being able to deal with different customers, khadija stated,

> I mean, it's like in any other organization. Yet it [the tourism industry] has a different way of dealing with customers. It's [tourism work] mostly face-to-face, trying to solve problems. First of all if you have an angry customer, so it [tourism employment] makes you take quick action, like solving problems and like listening to customers or like face to face, it's specific, and apart from that, yeah you do anything just to satisfy a customer, so.

Zuwena explained the need to be sociable and a "people person" when it comes to providing good customer service, "in terms of the tourism industry, you have to be very social, very outspoken, you have to be able to you know how to speak to both men and women". And Shariffa also talked about the importance of "personality", "it's yourself how you, you know how you, you, its about more about your personality also it does matter". Having a strong personality in terms of being confident, tough and strong was also emphasized by the women as necessary in order to work in the tourism industry. For example, Fatima explained the difficulty for women who felt they had to display a tough personality, which was difficult for women to do, "You need to be tough, I literally had to claw my way up (laughing) and go through so many things at the front desk as a female 'cause we are so emotional". Others also talked about the need to be strong or to have a strong personality. For example:

> .. Be strong and to know how to talk and how to present themselves
>
> (Nadia).

> Hotel work is more demanding, you can go wrong and everything would be on your head. And you need to consider some people if they make a mistake, it's coming out of your salary, ahhm. The image that you are giving out [being weak]: maybe the managers would not be happy with the outcome [the image] that you are giving [being an incompetent worker]. So it's all pressures

and it's all how you project [deal with difficult work situations]. And if you are having a bad day or bad mood, you cannot [show it]. You always need to have this smile on your face because sometimes it's difficult, it's difficult to keep [maintain a strong image] (Laila).

Furthermore, having the right attitude meant being patient, open minded, showing potential and having the willingness to work. For example,

> If you have the right attitude, if you've got the willingness... It's not going to be an easy road, you know. A lot of people had to start from scratch. I was just lucky that I didn't have to start from scratch. I started off already you know [with the right attitude]. You have to have patience you know, ahh you have to keep in mind that, you know. I am going to struggle for the first year or two and then eventually, I am going to gain the experience (Salwa).

> Hmmm, I think besides education wise, just to be open to [being open minded], to be able to work in groups, to hmm speak out, to not to be like... You don't have to be aggressive, but to be out there [be outgoing], you know (Aisha).

Overall, the first theme revealed that the women got involved in tourism employment as a result of various factors including chance, family encouragement and new tourism education opportunities in Oman. However, they also encountered some difficulties in obtaining employment because of high job competition, the preference for men in many jobs and lack of experience. In terms of tourism work, the women reported that the tourism industry seems to have particular expectations in terms of the "ideal candidate". This included having specific skills, personality and "attitude", such as being social, out-going and "tough".

Theme 2: Facing Negative Attitudes

Apart from the difficulties of obtaining a job in tourism, and dealing with the initial adjustment to the job situation, many of the women also had continued to face difficulties with some of the attitudes they encountered at work. The second theme focuses on the negative attitudes they faced from employers, society, family members, husbands and from themselves.

2.1 Employer's attitudes.

Many of the women reported that employers had negative attitudes to women workers because they were likely to get married and have children. Fatima described the perception that her employer had towards her and the expectation that she would not take her job seriously.

> They [employers] kept on thinking that I was going to quit at anytime, and I was going to go off and tell them that I am getting married, and if I did get married, I might get pregnant, and I am

just going to quit, you know and I wouldn't take it seriously because it's just a job, and I will be too dumb to do it [unable to perform the job], yeah.

Similarly, Salwa explained:

If you have too many Omani females in a department, it's a problem. Why? Because when she gets married, she needs a holiday, when she's pregnant, she needs a maternity leave, so therefore they [employers], avoid having them [having too many women employees].

Other examples included:

I guess, maybe not being taken seriously. If, let's say you have a higher position, maybe they [the employees] won't follow what you say or do what you ask your employee to do (Aisha).

I don't know if they [employers] think it's a threat [to hire women] or if they look and say Omani, she's going to get married and have children, and there will be problems with being pregnant every year (Zuwena).

Because of this, employers were seen to favor men who were thought to be more reliable and productive workers. Comments on this included:

Well, mostly with ahh, difficulties it's more of, [because of] being a woman. Sometimes in Oman, it's a bit, like working in general, they [employers] wouldn't hire women. I feel like it wasn't really [fair]. They would prefer a male to do certain jobs than a woman (Khadija).

I mean you have people that say, "I would prefer to hire a male", and I have heard stories ..., I know people [who hire men](Salwa).

The preference for male workers seemed to be also evident with customers preferring to deal with male workers over women workers, as explained by Laila,

Yes, hmm, I feel that if a customer approaches, especially men, they prefer to speak to men. Like if I am at the front desk and so is my colleague that turns out he is busy, they [customers] would approach me because I am the only one who is available but then they would start looking at my colleague and hoping to grasp his attention, to move the conversation towards him.

2.2 Society's attitudes.

Many of the women also discussed societal attitudes, and how these attitudes filtered down to their situations. For example, they talked about negative attitudes towards women working in places where alcohol was served, and where there would be international visitors. As Nadia said, "and you know especially in our culture, working in a hotel is a big thing [a big issue]. I mean, especially when it [involves] ... you know there's bars and guests, and international people". The women who chose to work in tourism often received negative comments about their employment because of working in this type of environment. Comments on this included:

> It was not taken [viewed] very well, I understand, you know, because females work in an industry that serves alcohol. And you are out there, meeting clients who are male, and you are going out [making sales calls], and you have to entertain males [made good sales calls with men]. It is not looked at very positively (Salwa).

> Yes, yes, you still get it, you get a bit like, "ohh you are working in a hotel" (laughing) (Khadija).

> Some of the people... Once you say you work at the hotel, their faces change. They expect . . . what they think is that if a woman works in a hotel, it's wrong. They just feel like it's not a good place. They think, "Ok she works in a place where they serve alcohol and this and this". Like you get that sometimes from other people (Munira).

2.3 Family members' attitudes.

In many Muslim societies, family members, such as mothers, fathers, and others have considerable influence on women's career decisions. For example, family members may be concerned about the type and conditions of the kind of work the women are involved with. Shift work, working late at night, inflexible schedules and specific work environments are often considered to be inappropriate. Khadija explains some of the problems that she encountered with her family because of her employment in a hotel:

> Ahhm, well, when I was studying... The truth is like they were supportive at the beginning, as it is a new field and everything. But then there were other things that were, of course, a bit hard to accept [for them]. Like not everybody in the family, but a few members of the family, would still not accept the idea of [me] working in a hotel, something like that.

The same situation occurred for Aisha, as she stated,"(laughing), for me it was fine [working late night], but since I live with my parents, my father had a problem if I was doing night shift". Other women also spoke about the way in which parents, in general, and particularly fathers, discouraged their daughters from working in the tourism field:

> I mean the father; the parents have a big role [influence on their daughters] providing advice. But if the parents' support is not there . . . if the parents are more conservative, the strength [of

the parents influence] will mean that the girls won't be able [to choose tourism employment], to be out there in hotels, so they choose a different area [career] (Nadia).

Yes, it could be an issue [work conditions] because some of them [family members], they don't accept that, their children they are...For example, for their daughter to be in a hotel industry, some of them they don't accept it (Munira).

2.4 Husband's attitudes.

Similar negative attitudes were evident among some of the women's husbands as well. Again, this was related to the type and conditions of work such as being on the front line, working long hours, shift-work, and various job obligations. The following women explained their husband's negative views towards their work in tourism:

Because of the working hours, because of the shifts you know. And I think, for me I don't see it [didn't agree], but I understand from their [husband's] point of view. My husband, he's Omani. I mean, yeah, he used to go to England every summer, but he's an Arab (Zuwena)

When I want to the airline, it was then he had to hold his breath because I was working 12 hours a day, from 6 am to 6 pm, plus I work at home, yeah, so he was like [unhappy about the working hours], he had to, you know, be more patient [with her work], you know" (Shariffa).

These attitudes were also of concern to single women when it came to future marriages, as Salwa explains,

It will be tough because I see it from my boss [who struggles with her husband's attitudes], 'ahh she's got two children and when she has to stay back, sometimes it's like, even if it's just for two hours you know, because we finish at 5 and she leaves at 7, three days in a row, she's already getting "yuk yuk yuk" from her husband, you know (laughing). I know it will be tough, not everybody will be able to understand that "ok, she works", you have to stay a bit longer but it's an image that you have to deal with right now, as it occurs (laughing).

Other women spoke about husbands being conservative and protective as well as not being understanding towards their wives' involvement in tourism employment. This made it more difficult for married women to work in the tourism industry. The following women talked about their husbands' influence and concerns for their wives' involvement in tourism employment:

A married woman it depends on her husband. Yeah like not everyone is understanding. "Well this is a job, even if she comes at night [from work], this is because of her job, and she's doing this because of this and this". No, some of them – husbands - they don't understand that. They just want like ahh... ok especially in a hotel as well. You deal with lots of men; there is this going on, doing all this; so not everyone understands. Some of them don't like it, but some of them they don't understand; they don't accept their wives to come back home late evening (Munira).

I understand Arab men tend to think of their wives as their possessions you know. And even if somebody is looking at the "possession" [their wives], it's hurtful for them (laughing). And when you are in the hotel industry, even if somebody is flirting with you, you can't be rude you see. And the idea is that they think "ohh this one, we met so and so's wife, she was laughing with us, she was smiling with us". For them [husbands], that's an offense [to flirt with customers]. It's almost as if you were entertaining the customers when you are actually just doing your job (Zuwena).

Similar to the previous section, the attitudes of family members and husbands reflected cultural beliefs and the need to maintain religious and cultural norms. As seen with both the family members' and husband's attitudes, there seems to be a belief in the need to protect their daughters' or wife's reputation and honor. This was seen to be a problem because of the demands of tourism work for women and the perception of inappropriate work conditions and environments.

2.5 Women's self-attitudes.

Not only do women encounter negative attitudes towards their work in tourism from society, family members and husbands, but the women themselves also had some negative attitudes towards tourism work. This is partly because of the cultural shock they experienced at the beginning of their careers in tourism employment and because of being unprepared for the work environment and pressure. Fatima explained the difficulties that Omani women encounter,

Mostly Omani women they can't [can't handle the pressure], especially if you come from a sheltered life or if your parents are close minded and they didn't tell you that this is what you have to do to get by [reality of work]. Then they just think, you know, that it's just a job. But if you think it's just a job and you are going to stand there at the desk, the first time you get a guest complaint, I have seen them [women] fall apart. They don't know what to do [how to handle the pressure of dealing with a complaint].

Specifically, when it comes to serving alcohol, some of the women talked about the difficulty that female waitresses encountered because of being unprepared to serve alcohol:

It's more of the idea was ..., like let's say during events – apart from restaurants and you know, and maybe nightclubs - apart from that, let's say during events, we have banquets, so we had a

> lot of Muslim women during that [banquets] as well. They were complaining that they didn't want to serve alcohol, but they had to because it's their job. So I felt sorry for them, like they are doing something that they are not happy about [serving alcohol]. They don't want to [serve alcohol] (Khadija).

> I think one of the things that they might come across that could be complicated is dealing with alcohol. So you see, that's another thing. If they do [serve alcohol], like if they serve the alcohol, that definitely would be a "no no" here for sure [not viewed positively by society] (Zuwena).

As explained in the last theme, the women were aware that they would need to have certain skills, personality and attitude in order to work in the tourism industry. However, many women do struggle at the beginning of their employment due to the job requirements. Fatima explained her own conflicting experience in trying to adapt to tourism work, which led to her to leave her first tourism job,

> Even though I was willing to learn - I was willing to work hard, I used to put a lot of hours in it - I just couldn't. I was really too young. I didn't t know then what I know now. I just did what every young person would do. I just left, quit, because I couldn't take it, I couldn't take the pressure.

The other problem lay with the women's lack of confidence and self esteem that made working in the tourism industry difficult. As some of the women explained,

> Ok, first of all, I was thinking "ohh my god, I think it's difficult, it's tough working in a hotel". And especially I was thinking of the shift, "Maybe I cannot handle it - finishing so late in the evening" (Munira).

> I don't like dealing with problems. I am a very reserved girl. I am very shy. I am in the wrong field, you know. I mean, I could be somewhere else, but just dealing with guests; I am not much of a talkative person, either (Laila).

> At the beginning, it wasn't easy. I was given [so much] information, listening and taking in information about the industry. I was lost" (Nadia).

It is possible that some women who 'try out' tourism employment often decide not to continue in this type of work because of these concerns and worries. Indications of this included,

> For example, when I used to work in the hotel, I met with Omani ladies who were coming for training at the hotel from the university and institute. Not a lot of them from the university. And

I asked them "what are [your goals]? You're really doing well, What are you going to do in future? What would you see yourself [doing in the future]?" And they might say "not hotels. I would maybe work in travel agencies". I ask them "why? I mean you are doing well, you had this customer orientation and you are very oriented and [trained well]". And the women said "No. The people are different. The people are drinking". And the women were afraid. They didn't want to [be seen by others], I mean they should [try tourism work], but they are just afraid (Nadia).

They [the women] are not taking advantage [of tourism work]. Yes, it depends on, the way you are - you know the way you think, your personality. Again, it's the religion, being near a male, it's there, in their minds you know. They would say "tourism work- I don't think its something to do with us [tourism work not being appropriate]" (Shariffa).

Yes, some of them [women working in tourism], I see the way they complain [about the work]. Some of them are working only because they want a job, and they need a salary, they need money, not because they are thinking of being something in the future or they have a target. No, [they think] "just come to work, do the job and get my salary". That's all. So it's like they only work because of that. They don't have any motivation. They have nothing [no ambition]. So and it's quite difficult for them, like working in shifts, especially [for] a girl (Munira).

The attitudes that some women have towards tourism employment may also have reinforced employers' negative attitudes towards women employees. Overall, this theme revealed the various negative attitudes that the women encountered in tourism employment. These included employers' negative attitudes towards female employment, and their belief that women did not make good employees, especially if they were married with children. The employers' views were linked to societal attitudes about female employment in the tourism industry and the inappropriateness of the tourism environment for women. Within the Islamic culture and within the Islamic society, there are wide spread concerns about the western style of tourism, for example, the involvement of alcohol and the serving of pork in various tourism establishments. Because of this, there have been issues related to the acceptance of tourism employment, especially with women working in environments that are viewed negatively. Further, these societal beliefs meant that the women often encountered negative attitudes from family members and from husbands. Moreover, although the women in this study were all still working in the tourism field, they all knew of other women who left this type of employment due to the various difficulties, negative attitudes, and or specific job requirements. The attitudes that were explored in this theme were not new to the women since they reflected common cultural and religious norms, and since all of the women had seen or been affected by negative attitudes towards tourism work for women.

Theme 3: Challenges of Tourism Work

Not only did the women experience various negative attitudes towards their work in the tourism industry, they also talked about a range of challenges that they faced associated with tourism employment.

3.1 The challenges of work conditions and demands.

In terms of work conditions, the women complained that having to work on holidays and weekends, and about long hours and hectic work schedules. Further, many did not receive compensation and had little flexibility with regards to vacation time. Comments on the working conditions included,

> Of the hours, it's like ten hours a day... meeting and dealing with customers, and being there in the front line... If your [shift] is coming to an end, lets say by 6 pm, you can't just go "ok I worked ten hours. No" (Nadia).

> I have been doing it [working in tourism] for almost two years now, and with no vacations, nothing. And I am just tired. I am still young (laughing), and if I feel like this now, and I am still not exactly at proper management [level], how will I feel later on? (Laila).

> Also during the weekends, the travel agency [her employer], they used to do some, some [weekend work] especially when in a tourism department. So sometimes on the weekend I do work (Shariffa).

> Well, lets say for Eid holiday... they would give us three days, while it's like, it's [often] four days. They will give us 3 days for Eid holidays and for public holidays. It depends on how busy we are. If we are busy, we have to work on that day, and then take some other time [off] (Khadija).

Much of the tourism work also had some required social obligations, where the women had to work outside of the office or attend work-related events after working hours or on the weekend. For example,

> So you have to attend social events, you know, the embassy is throwing a dinner party-national day, you know. Even though you're working hours are 8 to 5, you have to attend these events for networking purposes (Salwa).

> No, I didn't have to do shifts. My shift was from 8 to 5, but 6 days a week. But then, lets say when we have an event happening, sometimes we have to attend the event (Khadija).

> We have to attend a lot of conferences, you know, every time you get a visitor from X or Y country. They have to show us their products. It is a full day conference, we have to be there, you know. Or sometimes we have to organize a presentation, for a full month just presenting our product. There again [sometimes] you have to go out. And if you go out, that means you have to go with your boss. You have to go with your supervisor (Shariffa).

Because of the working conditions, the women found that they had less time for attending family get-togethers, compared to jobs with standard work hours. They talked about missing family gatherings held on weekends and holidays. Fatima said, "You know we Omanis are very family oriented. [The job] kind of took me away from that. I couldn't spend much time with the family". Khadija explained about being unhappy with having less time with her family, which resulted in her having to leave her hotel work,

> When I was working in the hotel, I really felt sort of left out, or something like that. I felt that 'cause I didn't have time [for my family]. It was all about work, and I wasn't happy. I couldn't balance [work and] family. I mean they [the family] were there, but I wasn't there (Khadija).

Aisha described having no social life,

> Definitely, it affects [me]. It depends what day of the week you have off. It won't necessarily be the weekend. And I think it's hard to do a lot for your family on that one day [off], especially if you just want to relax or just enjoy, ... because I noticed coming back home, I didn't want to do anything right after my shift. I just wanted to stay at home and relax, so [I] hardly went out. You don't have a social life basically (laughing).

The women also found that the high pace, the standards and the expectations of tourism work also presented challenges. They often had many tasks at the same time, which they had to manage as best they could.

> It was ahh hectic. It was very fast paced. Even like, you know, you have your break, [but] you wouldn't take it cause you have so much work to do. Or you wouldn't take the full hour [full break]. You would just go quickly for half an hour and then come back (Aisha).

They [the hotels] have very high expectations and they basically don't care. I mean they actually tell you "you are manager, and you have to work these hours, you have no choice" (Fatima).

Because of working [in the past] for two different properties [two hotels], there are some people who expect you to be there [all the time]. I mean, you are expected to entertain your clients, at least twice a week. So you put into your mind that twice a week. I am going to have to stay [stay late] (Salwa).

This hectic pace and work pressure resulted in the women feeling stressed, frustrated and overwhelmed. Laila described her stress and frustration in this way, "Sometimes it's too much. Sometimes I feel just like closing my ears and walking out (laughing). Towards the end [of the day], it becomes too much". Fatima also experienced similar frustrations and stress and said, "They drained me, yeah. They literally drained me. I am exhausted. This is what I was looking for. I was looking for a challenge. Now I have a challenge, but it's ridiculous the way they work there".

3.2 The challenges of progressing in tourism work.

The women who had progressed into the higher-level positions in the tourism industry found that the demands and challenges had actually increased even more. They reported additional stress and frustration. As Nadia said,

When I was the supervisor, I used to leave between 4 and 5. When I was promoted to a manager, and [became] the group coordinator, I stayed really late. We had groups coming in, let's say even the delegation, king and queen and all that. I had to be there. I was there. I used to stay there to make sure that the arrival was great. We met them on their arrival, so I had to, you know, I stayed really late.

Salwa explained the various responsibilities that her high level position required her to do,

I am the assistant director of sales and marketing. My job requires me to look after different things. I look after the ministry. I look after the tour operators. I look after the advertising and marketing of the hotel. So yeah, I am juggling. Normally it's 3 different people doing this job (laughing), but because we are a smaller property, it's combined into one person.

Similar concerns were also evident for women seeking promotion in tourism work. These women felt that they had to "prove themselves" to be promoted. Comments included:

I need to work hard and to prove to them that I can do this, I can handle this, to show them...not to give them the chance [to deny my promotion] when I request to move to this department (Munira).

> That's one of the reasons they don't take women as duty managers, because it's a tough job [for women] to do (Fatima).

> Yeah, between studying and working at the hotel, it's almost 9 years. So [after] 9 years I should take a managerial position. People were coming in with [work experience]-I don't know how many [years of experience]-and they didn't even have their studies. So when I went there [to the management], of course I demanded [a promotion] (Zuwena).

The women also felt that they were discriminated against, in terms of promotion, because of the preference for men in higher-level positions. This also increased the stress level for women seeking promotion. For example,

> Ahh, you have to…I had to prove myself to them, and show them that I am serious and I know what I am talking about. And it's very different because they are used to a male, an Omani male, you know. With a male, [they] are more comfortable, [they] can talk about whatever they want. They can go out drinking or whatever. There's a disadvantage [for] the female (Salwa).

> Because of the pressure [work pressure], the pressure is too much. And the funny thing is that if you look at it in Oman, there are more males, men working in the high level positions than there are women [Fatima].

> I think in general, I mean I noticed most of the managers in hotels are men. It's very [unlikely] that you find a lady who is a manager or what ever. I have never seen a general manager who is a lady, for example, although I have a lot of women who are ambitious to reach that level, I haven't seen it yet (Laila).

3.3 The challenges of being a working wife and mother.

Women who were married or married with children also faced the challenge of balancing work and family, and being able to fulfill their family responsibilities. In addition, the attitudes of husbands towards tourism employment made it more challenging for the women to be a working wife and mother, as discussed in the previous theme. Nadia, a mother of two children, put it this way, "because my mind will be with my kids, I will be thinking about them. Working long hours…no, I mean, if I was single, I would perform, perform more. I would be more productive than if I am married with two kids. This is me". Munira, who was just recently married, explained "it's too difficult and it's too hard [balancing work and marriage] especially like now…I just got married in August, it was 19th of August, so I found it quite different-when I was single compared to now".

The single women were also aware of the challenges that they may encounter when they get married and have children. Comments from single women included,

> Yes, especially if I do decide to work in a hotel, hmmm, shift work will be the most [challenging]-the biggest problem. Especially if you have children, they are going to school, when will you see them? And then it also depends on your husband - how open he is to you working late night shifts. It's definitely an issue (Aisha)

> It would be more difficult [marriage and children] because not a lot of people [employers] will be understanding and not a lot of people will care. I mean in this job, I don't care what hotel or company [it is] or whatever, it will be difficult. As a married woman, you would have other obligations... you have your husband to attend to; you have your children (Laila).

3.4 The challenge of discrimination against local employees.

Another challenge faced by the women was that of discrimination against local employees. The reliance on expatriates to fill tourism jobs is still practiced, despite the encouragement for Omani women to work in the tourism industry. This is probably because the Oman tourism industry is still fairly new and relies on foreign expertise for developing the Oman tourism industry. Although having expatriates was beneficial because of their training and work knowledge, it also caused some problems, specifically for Omani women. One problem is the competition with expatriates. The women in this study talked about competing with expatriates, and being at a disadvantage in terms of speaking English, educational level, and work experience.

> They [management] think a white face in the front office shows that we have professional people in our work industry. I think that's the only logical explanation why somebody would do that [hire expatriates]. Where as I am thinking, "ok English, well I speak English just as well as they do". I already studied [hospitality and tourism]. Work experience, I already have work experience. And if you look at my training theme [training record].You [management] could not send me abroad if I didn't have a very good training record (Zuwena).

> I was the first Omani. I was the first female Omani. And they were all male. They were all Indians. And there was one other female woman. She was Indian. So you can imagine the situation I was put in. I was Omani. They didn't like it because they were afraid that I might take their job because of Omanisation (Fatima).

A second problem revolved around expatriates not understanding the cultural values of the Omani society, particularly the significance of family, and the demands of family on women. This was evident in terms of certain work conditions and demands and problems related to working late at night or working on weekends, etc. The cultural clash with expatriates made it more difficult for women to perform their jobs well. Laila encountered a cultural clash with an expatriate in management when it came to working the late night shift,

> I told them [expatriate in management] that I cannot work night shifts. My parents don't agree. I don't agree. And they [expatriate in management] are like "why?" They even had to ask me. I said it's a cultural thing. We do not work [night shifts]. We do not stay outside the house you know [till late at night]. And they found it difficult to accept, which I found uncomfortable. Because you [expatriates in management] are coming here [to Oman], you should know the culture and how things work here.

Other comments on the cultural clash between expatriates and the women included,

> Ahh no, with the German ladies I mean, for example, they always have an attitude. This is how they are raised. They are more different. They are different from Omanis (Nadia).

> You know, that's the wrong kinda of thing [wrong thinking of expatriates]. And she [expatriate colleague] was very much like, "you know, in Europe and in Germany we do this [different methods of working]". But I said, "We are not in Germany. You have to understand, you have to adapt to the Omani culture. You have to adapt to the Arabs" (Zuwena).

3.5 The challenge of being on the front line.

Tourism work is often associated with providing good customer service and being able to deal with different people. The women found that being on the "front line" in terms of mixing with men and dealing with difficult customers was an additional challenge. As Fatima explained, "It's a hotel that has bars, and there are people that come to stay there, and like go to the bar and drink. And to be on the front line you have to deal with men all the time". Shariffa explains,

> Plus they [women] do talk with a lot of customers - guys. And you know here in our country like "ohh you cannot talk to you know [men], even if it's your work. You just have to do your work. You have to be careful". Not only that, they [Omani women] agree there is a mix [of genders], but as long as you do your work, and they do their work. But here, no. I might be just sitting, waiting, I could meet today a guy, maybe 10 to 15 guys in a day you know. [I might] give him a number, [he might] call me at the office. If they are traveling abroad, I have to you know, provide them with the mobile number in case of having any problems [travel problems]. [This is when] we face the problems with our family.

This was further compounded when customers were "difficult". For example, Laila said "Yeah, they [customers] can be very difficult, and they blame you for things [when] they know that it's not your fault. The municipality cuts water faucets, all of a sudden it's your fault, and you get screamed at and blamed. [And you] can't say anything". And Aisha explained further, "It's a very very tough job, and I don't think you get recognition for it, hmm, especially from guests sometimes. It's - I wouldn't say it's abuse, but it's just they feel superior to you, and I guess that's what I didn't like".

3.6 The challenge of low pay.

As discussed in the literature review, the tourism industry is well known for it's low pay. This, along with low recognition for a difficult job, was also a challenge that the women faced. The concern was not only that the pay was low, but also that the pay scale was perceived to be particularly unfair, given the work conditions and demands. As Laila said,

> Pay is very low. Because of the amount of work you go through and the amount of stress you go through, at the end of the day, it's peanuts [paycheck is low]. Sometimes, I mean in [other] bigger industries, they over work, they do overtime. And some of them [other industries], they do two or three shifts. And it depends on what type of job you are doing in your industry, but the pay is not what you expect [in the tourism industry].

Fatima also described her frustration with low pay, "Yes, hotel industries. Their pays [salaries] are ridiculous. You do such a tough job and you get the worst pay, ...no one has done nothing about it, and somebody should do something about it". Zuwena further states, "I worked very hard for peanuts, you know, we work sometimes, 6 or 7 days a week". The low pay and low recognition was also seen to contribute to the general high turnover in the tourism industry. For example,

> It's a bit like, not really encouraging people to work in a hotel. Because after working long hours, and after all the hard work, and you don't really get paid... you are not paid what you deserved. I think that's a bit [unfair] (Khadija).

> I mean in general, generally, tourism you know has a high turn over of employees because of the [low] salary. That's, ...one of the challenges (Nadia).

> One of the problems that a lot of hotels are facing is turnover of Omanis. What happens is, especially a smaller property that hires an Omani that is fresh from school or from college...a trained one - and they would stay for an average of 4 to 5 month. And than a bigger hotel would come and snatch them away because of 50 rials extra and they would go (Salwa).

Yes, if you have job satisfaction, you can retain your staff, I don't think you will suffer from high turnover. I think one of the major problems is a lot of people don't have job satisfaction and than eventually, they kinda of leave out of frustration, and so on and so forth (Zuwena).

Thus the interviews revealed a range of difficulties facing Oman women working in the tourism industry. These related not only to the low pay, but also to the long hours, high stress and evening and weekend work. This made it difficult for the women to balance work and family. Moreover, work expectations often affected cultural norms, for example expectations of serving alcohol and mixing and interacting with male employees and customers, adding to the stresses and challenges of the work situation.

Theme 4: Dealing with Negative Attitudes and Challenges

All of the women in this study were still working in the tourism industry despite the many challenges they faced. They had found ways to deal with these challenges, including the challenges of the work environment, of their family responsibilities, and of the negative attitudes they faced.

4.1 Accepting, adapting and finding strategies to address challenges.

In terms of work challenges, many of the women dealt with this challenge through a combination of accepting, adapting and finding strategies to improve their situation. In terms of accepting the situation, the women tried to develop a positive outlook on their work, and a determination to work hard in order to be successful. Munria recalled,

So from the first, before I started [tourism employment], I was like "oh my god I feel it's really difficult". Then I just kept one thing in my mind "Nothing is impossible, so let's try. Why not? Why do others [successed]? What is so special [about] them?" So let me try. Maybe it will work with me. I did not expect that it would work with me. So [later] I was like, "I like it" [tourism employment].

Fatima recalled changing her attitude towards her work. She said, "it was intimidating but because I changed for it [adapted to it]. The most critical time was doing the night shift".

Accepting and adapting to the situation required deploying various techniques and strategies. One was simply getting used to the routine by not giving up. Aisha said, "I guess yes, after a while, you adapt to it. Maybe I wouldn't like it from the beginning, but as I said, it becomes routine, and you get used it". Similarly, Shariffa said,

I got used to the time and everything. And especially if you, start to, you know, meet different people, and start to talk about the travel and arrangements, the time is just going [time flies] and you feel like "ohh I didn't finish yet with this person". And you know, "I need to sit more, you need to tell him more about it", and the time you know keeps [flying by].

Another strategy involved working hard, doing the best job they could and improving their skills and competences. Shariffa commented on how she managed the demands of her work, "as long as I have the information, I study my product very well, then I build up my [confidence]-the confidence to go out and, you know, and start to talk about it". Salwa managed by multi tasking, "It's juggling. It's a lot of juggling, you know, because I, you have to put in a 100% effort in all different aspects of your job. It's difficult but you manage, one way or the other".

As for progressing in tourism work, some of the women were able to get promoted and advance in their career by proving themselves to be competent. Salwa stated, "So you can move, you don't have to be in the same position for 2 to 3 years. You know you excel, and you know you are doing a good job, you can, absolutely". Khadija kept a positive attitude about being able to progress by taking up opportunities to improve her level of competency, "Ahh, like in personal development and growing. So I think it depends, from one person to another, what their perspective is. But for me, it was, 'if this is what I want, sure, there is a chance to prove yourself [to the management]'. It doesn't matter if it's the tourism industry or anything else". Fatima learned to accept the work conditions and demands in order to be a duty manager, "no no no, I wanted it. I was like 'If I was going to be a duty manager, I wanted to be a proper duty manager', I wanted to go through the night shift as well". Munira described how she learned to handle difficult work situations. She talked about dealing with an angry customer when she was unable to process his credit card payment due to technical delays:

> So I just took it as usual. And so at times like that ...you have to know how are you going to deal with that situation, how you are going to handle it. So it's simple, I didn't take it personally. I just took the money and continued with my job. And still, I did apologize to him for the delay. [I was just] normal. And on the second day, god forgive me, in two days, he sent a letter to the front office manager, thanking and apologizing [for being rude].

The women found other strategies when it came to dealing with issues such as schedules. Specifically, some of the women were able to negotiate with the management to reach an agreement that fit better with their needs. Munira explained how she negotiated with the management to find a schedule that allowed her to attend evening classes at the college:

> Well, what I did, I made a request to the management. Yeah, like those days I had classes [evening classes], I needed morning shifts, yeah. So it's like in a week, four days I have a morning shift and the rest whatever shifts they can give, I am fine [doing other shifts].

Similarly, Laila was also able to negotiate with the management for her schedule. She said "They [management] were fine because I have been studying it [French classes] for [a long time]. This is my... I am going into my third year. So I told them from before that I have twice a week French classes that I cannot miss".

4.2 Making choices with regards to child related issues.

When it came to child related issues and being a working mother, the women found a variety of ways of dealing with this challenge. Many of the women talked about the challenges of balancing work and family responsibilities, and how they felt torn between their work and family responsibilities. One woman planned to quit work once she had children,

> I always tell [myself] when I have children; I want to be a house [wife]-a full time mother. When the children go to school, I will consider working again. So to me, between work and being a mother, I choose being a full time mother (Laila).

Another women left her demanding job position for a more flexible job position because of her children,

> I left the hotel last year... it's a point where I have to be with [my children]. It's a point where I choose my career over my kids. It's not that I won't work. It's just the hours were really inconvenient for me [at my previous job]; they were not convenient (Nadia).

Other women talked about only being willing to do certain types of tourism work that allowed them to spend at least some time with their children,

> No,... I would not go for a place where you have longer working hours and less holidays or something like that - that you can't spend [time] with your family. I mean I don't mind working in the tourism industry. I love it and everything.
>
> But [only if tourism employers] consider our family [having more time with family], we [get] two days off and the working hours are [flexible], you know (Khadija).

Despite the difficulties of managing both work and family, some of the women were determined to have a career and find a way to balance these two aspects of their lives. As a single woman, Fatima recognized the challenge, but wanted to find a way to continue working once she had children:

> I think when I get kids, that will be a different story. Yeah ok, you try maybe as much as you can to keep certain hours so that you can be at home with the kid [for part of the day]. But then, again, it's your job, life goes on.

Shariffa, a mother of two, found a different way of balancing work and family through working at home.

> So at home, at least, if I take work at home, I [can] leave work early so I can spend time with my kids. Although they sleep early. So if I get home late, then I don't get to see them... So the only thing [is that I try to] take my work home, for two to three hours maximum, I can sit with

them, play, a little fun. Because I need to refresh myself also before going back to work again (laughs).

Despite the women having different approaches, they all tried to find ways to achieve some sense of balance. As Salwa said, "it [is] more difficult [when] you have got two responsibilities. You don't only have one. However you know, you have to try and manage, you have to".

4.3 Accepting and conforming to employers' and societal attitudes.

Many of the women had found ways to deal with the negative attitudes at their workplace. Comments included:

> Well, it's a bit sad that there are people who still think like that. Hmm, well, I am sure a lady...she can still prove herself and she can work in any [job], I don't think there is any difference between a male and [a female] in terms of career wise and things like that (Khadija).

> I mean I didn't take anything really to heart. You know for me, I just...I really enjoyed my job; you know I loved the people who I was working with. They taught me a lot (Zuwena).

The women seemed to feel that there was nothing they could do to change some attitudes. Thus they had to learn to accept them as part of the cultural and religious setting of their society, which led to the favoring of men over women in the work place. The women attempted to conform to cultural standards of appropriate behavior as best as they could when it came to their work in tourism and sought to avoid or reduce negative attitudes towards them when possible. As Shariffa stated, this meant representing herself appropriately when it came to dealing with male customers:

> It's just...you know, how you...how you present [yourself], how you talk to them [male customers] or how you [deal with male customers]. I don't know cause I feel like if you...if you do respect yourself and you know...It's not that "No, if I don't talk to him [male customer] or if I don't you know, do this with him together [help a male customer]". You know, I mean I [don't] cross the line of my religion and all that. No, it's just a matter of you know... how you present yourself - whether you talk with him [male customers], whether you joke with them. Everything, you know, has a limit and it's you, it's all about you [to determine that limit].

Similarly, Salwa explained the importance of covering her head and dressing appropriately when it came to making sales calls with Omani male clients. While she laughed at this requirement, she also saw it as necessary because of prevailing "negative attitudes".

> Trust me, if I was not wearing this [her scarf]...I started wearing this because of going to the ministries. If I didn't (laughing), I would be in trouble. I mean, when I am not seen dressed in a skirt. Other wise they would eat you alive (laughing). No, it's still, I mean negative. Definitely.

4.4 Attempting to change family members' and husbands' attitudes.

In comparison, the women did seek to change the attitudes of their family members by trying to emphasize the importance of their work. Shariffa described how her family tried to persuade her to choose a business administration career over tourism. But she tried to convince her family of the value of tourism employment and they came to accept it:

> Then they [her family] were pushing me to study business administration, you know. They said this [business administration field] is more [appropriate]. And [I] wanted to travel, to study [tourism]. So they said "There is no future in it" [in tourism employment]. But I did try you know, to talk to them. And then they said "ok fine. If you feel like, you want to try, just go ahead and see how is it". And then, after some time, then they came to know that it's really good [a good form of employment].

Salwa explained how she tried to convince her mother that her choice of tourism employment was a good one. Her mother was hesitant at the beginning because of her concerns on the work conditions and how society would view her daughter:

> And my mother was a bit hesitant, initially, you know. And it took a lot of convincing (laughing). And she still is, she still is [hesitant]. I understand she worries because of the outsiders [societal attitudes]...she sees it [tourism employment] from the outsider's eyes. And than she thinks..."I am not so sure if she [Salwa] works late, she leaves work late" you know. But I think to some extent it's changing [from what] it used to be five years ago.

However, it was not always possible for the women to change family members' attitudes. The women from strict families found this to be much more difficult than those from liberal families. For example, Fatima said, "My parents are very supportive because they are unlike a lot of Omanis. They are very open minded". And Zuwena commented,

> I think the people who have been exposed more [liberal ideas] are different from people from the village [who] are less exposed. You know, people who have been exposed more, or who have lived in the capital, and their children have studied abroad or the children have been to private schools - their way of thinking is different from those who went to government schools or those who are living in a village.

Laila expressed the difference between her family members who were not "strict" compared to some of her female colleagues who came from strict families.

> My family, they are not very strict. They are not strict at all. They are open-minded. But I have seen from my other [female colleagues]...I had an old colleague in my old hotel, and her parents were very strict. And if she had to do a night shift, it would be this big event that is

going on [problems with her family]. And her brother would have a problem that "You cannot do this, you cannot work [late nights]". So it was a problem for her.

Similarly, Aisha explained the restrictions that other women's families placed on them when it came to the working conditions of tourism employment:

> Like, for instance, when I was studying here at the college. We had a lot of girls who came from the interior, who were not from the capital basically. And I was [surprised], you know, their parents put a lot of restrictions on them. And I was wondering how would that help them in an industry like this because it's... you have to be flexible, especially in hotels, you are going to be doing shift work.

Some of the women also sought to change the attitudes of their husbands, in order to gain support and understanding for their tourism employment. For example, Shariffa was already working in the tourism industry when she got married, and she wanted the support of her husband for her form of employment.

> Hmmm, at the beginning [of her marriage], it was difficult. Because, again, I am sitting there, talking with everybody you know [male customers], laughing and smiling. I have to be out by midnight for a meeting or something. Then again, another issue, another problem was [working late]. Then, after that, then as long as there was an understanding [between herself and her husband] and success [in her work], then it was ok after that.

Interestingly, the women who were not married at the time of the interview were also very aware of the importance of having a husband who was open-minded and supportive of their career choice. Comments included,

> I think about that [possible conflict with a future husband who might not be supportive], I do. I really do think about that. But then it depends... If you get a husband [who is] supportive, you can manage through it [working in tourism employment] (Fatima).

> Well the best thing [would be], when you get married... [to have] an understanding person and [one who understand what] your target is. What I mean is... you have a target [career target] and you need to reach that place. Yeah, so if he understands that, that ok she's suffering [work constraints] and at least one day she needs something [understanding], she's looking for something. So if he understands, then "thank god, and thanks to him [her husband] as well, because he understands my situation" (Munira).

Absolutely, I mean whoever my partner is going to be, he's gonna have to accept it [her tourism work], no doubt it (Salwa).

Two of the women had a husband who worked in the tourism industry as well. This was seen as an advantage because their husbands were more likely to accept their tourism work. One married women described meeting her husband in a hotel, where they both worked, and how it helped for both of them to work in the same industry. She described this situation in the following way:

Maybe they met there and they are both open minded. They know about tourism. They know what is expected from [their work]. It's, you know, jealousy and doing things [in tourism employment], you know these things doesn't count there [doesn't matter for couples working in the tourism industry]. Work is the main thing [between the couple] and what you have to achieve by the end of the day. And my husband is very open-minded. He loves working in hotels. We met in hotels.

Munira's husband also worked in the tourism industry. She said "He's in the airport, working for an airline. Yeah, so he got shift [work] as well, so it's like we both understand each other".

Thus, this theme revealed the various ways that the women dealt with the attitudes and challenges they faced due to their employment. When it came to dealing with work related challenges, the women developed a combination of acceptance, adaptation and finding strategies. For example, they worked hard, tried to be positive, to do a good job and to negotiate with management. When faced with the challenge of being a working mother, some decided not to work after having children. Others wanted to purse their tourism career, but tried to negotiate for better working hours, or permission to work from home. With regard to societal attitudes and attitudes of employers, the women felt they had to accept these constraints, and to conform to expectations as best they could in an acceptable manner in terms of behavior and dress. However, the women were more proactive when it came to the attitudes of husbands and family members, in that they consciously tried to change negative attitudes towards their chosen form of work. They recognized that this was much easier for women whose husbands and other family members had more liberal, open-minded attitudes.

Theme 5: Importance of Tourism Work in Women's Lives

Despite the various negative attitudes and challenges associated with tourism work, most of the women in this study wanted to continue in their chosen career. They saw tourism work as an important part of their lives, and something that provided a number of benefits.

5.1 Enjoying tourism work.

The enjoyment of tourism work came largely from the opportunities it offered to meet and interact with people from different parts of the world, and to build confidence. Comments included,

It's very nice. I mean the good part of it [tourism employment]..., it's nice cause when you meet the tourists and you interact with them, you find a lot of nice people who appreciate what you are doing. When you are being appreciated, you feel really happy and when somebody thanks you. You know, "thank you" is more than enough because they know you did your best (Laila).

I enjoyed talking with [different people]. I thought that...[after] 11 years experience or 7 years experience of talking to the customer, I would be this tired; I would need a change and all that. But no, believe me, I really enjoy talking more [with customers] because also I think I [gain a lot] from them...I do learn a lot, I do learn a lot from them, and I do get something too [enjoyment] (Shariffa).

Like in hotel industry 'cause I am a person who likes dealing with the hotel you know cause I feel it's a place... to meet different people, you get to know different [people]. I mean you meet lots of nationalities and it's very nice you know (Munira).

In general, the women seemed to enjoy and be committed to their work. Salwa said, "I just wanted a job, I feel in love with the hotel industry after a while being in it". Similarly, Nadia said how she valued her work, "Because I like tourism, I love what I am doing, I am a people person".

5.2 Learning new skills.

Meeting and interacting with different people at work helped the women to improve their English language skills. For example, Nadia said, "I developed my English, you know . . . it wasn't that [it was bad]. It was fine, but I think meeting and dealing and talking every day, it helped a lot". Other interactional skills also developed, such as developing "people skills" and dealing with different and sometimes difficult people. Examples of comments included:

For me, I thought the experience was very good. It taught me a lot of people skills at a very young age because at 18, I had to attend these cocktail receptions; I had no idea how to talk to these people. You know, I went to my boss and I said, "look, I watch MTV and stuff like that. What am I going to talk to these middle aged and older people about?". He said, "No no no, you learn to make small talk, kind of thing". And it did [work]. I think that's why I think everyone should do it [tourism employment]. Because [some people think], "ohh I don't want to talk to people that I don't know".

Ahh, I needed to learn how to deal with customers. Like I improved in terms of how to deal with a guest complaint, you know...the tactics needed to speak to a guest in order to calm them down. I mean that you will learn in any department,... but specifically in the front office because you are dealing more with guest complaints (Laila).

Yes, I mean I am glad that I worked in a hotel. I learned a lot of things I must say. Like I learned, of course, a lot of things at the hotel industry. I can start by saying, like first of all, the experience of dealing with different customers (Khadija).

So that's the good thing-why I like working in a hotel industry. It really teaches you a lot - to know about people, to know their personality, their culture, the way they live, the way they are (Munira).

Other types of skills development were also mentioned, including leadership, time management and various technical skills,

They [the employers] did give us a lot, in fact, a lot of training. It helped us, like something like time management, you know, marketing yeah. In sales and marketing, there was a lot [of training]. Apart from customer service, they did give us like [more]. They gave me a course also, you know, in [doing] presentations (Shariffa).

Of course, like writing skills, knowing how to use computers, email, knowing how to make action plans, all the writing skills from a to z, I learned that in the hotel. We did a lot of training. We did like time management. We did leadership [training] (Nadia).

It was really tough and hard work and all, but it was very good for me, because I learned a lot through the training skills, through everything (Munira).

Not only had the women gained good practical skills but many of these skills were transferable to other job situations, Thus, enhancing their career opportunities and making them better candidates for future job options. As Fatima explained,

Yes I do, I believe that [that tourism employment is beneficial]. I mean it's not just about checking in or checking out a guest. I used to think that, you know. I mean the skills that we learn here, are going to help us in the future. You will be surprised, on the day-to-day basis, what we go through. And, you know, that I think these are skills that everyone needs.

Aisha also believes that she has gained work experience, which would enhance her future career options:

Hmm, professionally, I've now got something on my CV, which is always very important... that you have some sort of work experience. Hmm, and also I had a look at the different [areas of tourism employment]... like the events side of it, or the travel agency where I worked before, and also the hotel.

As for Salwa, learning new skills led to a decision to stay in the tourism field. She said, "exactly, yeah, it's something that I know how to do you know, so I might as well stick to what I know (laughing), but I would say it's a blessing you know, cause at least now I know".

5.3 Increased strength, confidence, independence and status.

In addition to gaining new skills and because of those new skills, many of the women felt that their employment in tourism work had helped them feel stronger, more confident and more independent. Shariffa described her confidence in being able to talk with different people after being exposed to difficult situations, where she had to use communication and problem solving skills, "first of all, it did build my strength, confidence yeah. The second thing, you know in terms of talking to [people], for me now [confident to talk to people]". Other comments included:

> I needed, first of all, I needed to develop - develop my confidence, I wanted to be more stronger. And since my English [improved] and myself also, my self-esteem is better, more confident (Nadia).

> I became stronger 'cause you are more exposed to the real world, you are more exposed to how to handle things (Laila).

> For myself, I feel it's a place that you can develop yourself. You get, yeah you will be open minded, deal with lots of things, lots of people, lots of, I mean different things yeah. So it's really a good place to develop yourself (Munira).

As for independence, this was related to economic independence for the women, and having their own income. As Zuwena said,

> That [working] made me feel very independent. Meaning I really didn't have [money]. I couldn't spend it without my parents asking "what do you want it for?". So that created a thing for me to like "Ohh I think I like working", because if I just want to spend my money on anything [I like], I can, 'cause it's mine. So it's fun (Zuwena).

However, another important aspect of independence was associated with learning to solve problems and to make independent decisions. Comments included;

> Because working in general, you feel you are independent, you know...working in general, no matter what. And working in the tourism industry, ahhmm, I think because you are just on your own there...you're on your own, and nobody treats you like a child. You don't know what you

are going to be [facing]. And your parents don't know how to tell you how to face [difficult] circumstances. So as I said, when you are facing a problem in the hotel. For example, nobody tells you what you are supposed to do: you are on your own. Even when you are supervised, as I said before, you learn how you can solve a problem, because you are always on your own, so you are totally on your own (Laila).

Furthermore, several of women felt they had gained status in terms of being part of something important. They felt proud of being part of the tourism industry and promoting their country. Fatima stated,

I feel very important. I feel very proud that I stuck with this industry. I felt very important that I reached the place that I reached [promotion]. It's more than just a job right now. It goes beyond that. I feel that I play a major role in the country's economy because I work in the hotel industry (Fatima).

Similarly, Khadija described how her work in tourism meant that she was representing her country, "Hmm, it's more of, …to me it's like representing your country. Like it's all about hospitality and we are known for our hospitality as you know. It's to represent our country of course". Shariffa also stated that leaving a good impression with a previous tour employer, made her feel important:

And believe me, still today, people [her former employer and customers] they are missing me out there. They say, "where is she? She was something [a good employee]" and I was like "No I was just doing my job", and they said "no, you are not". And every time they call me [customers still call her], I say "others can help [other current employees can help] but thank you for this [for remembering me]". And I get a lot of gifts [from customers]. And [her previous customers say] "no come back and this and that" [come back to your old job because you were very good], but I said, "I was just doing my job". They said, "no, you were doing more than you were" [going beyond her job] (laughing).

One woman even described her experience of working in tourism as one of "empowerment". She said,

In terms of confidence, 100% much much better. Empowerment, as I told you, you know I am in the position where you know; I bring money to [to the hotel]. I mean, I mean like wow, even the owner sometimes comes and says "thank you, fantastic job" [being appreciated], what more can I ask for (laughing). You know, if you are recognized by the owner of the hotel, you are recognized by the regional office, wow, yes, it's amazing (Salwa).

5.4 Having life changing experience.

Given the skill learning, and the gains in strength, confidence, independence and status, it is perhaps not surprising that many of the women saw their work in the tourism industry as a life changing experience. Munira talked about becoming a different person:

> This is what I think about myself yeah...like how I am now, and how I was before. Like the information I had before [versus] what I have now - it completely changed. The way I used to deal with people, the way I used to be, yeah. And now I feel it's completely changed [me]-what I used to have and now - everything has changed.

Similarly, Nadia also expressed having a life changing experience,

> Yeah, yeah, I was a very uneven [not outgoing] girl at first. I was very shy and very quiet, and I wouldn't be the way I am now if I had not worked in a hotel. Ahh, it taught me a lot of things. They sent me to Germany for exposure. I learnt a lot. I am a different person now. I mean I have seen different people, different behaviors, and you know all the training ... has made me a different person.

And Fatima said, "You do think that you never thought you had it in you to do. You become stronger. You become hmm more patient".

In summary, this theme revealed how tourism work became highly important in the women's lives after dealing with the various challenges they had faced. The women enjoyed and valued their work despite the negative attitudes and challenges. They enjoyed interacting with others and learning new skills, and many of these skills were transferable to other job situations. The enjoyment and skill learning led to increased confidence, strength, independence and status. In fact, several of the women talked about their tourism employment as being a life changing experience, which allowed them to become a different person.

Theme 6: An Expanded Vision of Tourism Work

Through their discussion of the difficulties and benefits of tourism employment, it was evident that the women's view of tourism work had changed dramatically since they first thought about this form of employment. Thus theme 6 focuses on the women's expanded vision of tourism work, going beyond their initial view of tourism as a regular job. This new vision includes a broader perspective of tourism work, a growing opportunity for the Omani tourism industry, a growing opportunity for women, and the need of better training and resources.

6.1 Gaining a broader perspective of tourism work.

Shariffa described tourism employment in terms of providing quality service. She said:

> Ahh, if I talk about [tourism work], it's all about the good things. Being in the tourism, ..., its not just about sitting there and selling tickets, ... and, you know, increasing the budget. No, it's about, ...your attitude, the way you think, the way you treat that client.

Others talked about tourism work as being exceptional in terms of what it included, and what it offered to employees. Examples included,

> Tourism covers a lot of things, unlike other specialized industries. Tourism deals with management skills, you know, they deal with practical, they deal with cooking, you deal with engineering cause if you have to build, you have engineering in the hotel, so you are, they deal with accounts. So they cover a variety of things where some organizations don't (Zuwena).

> Yes, I think tourism is more flexible. I think this could be because, as I said, it's seasonal. And ..., I think it's more flexible because you are not restricted to just one place (Laila).

> I mean I started [realizing] from when I was working in the hotel. When I started working and I opened my eyes and it was like "Wow. This is a totally different environment. Its fun, challenging, meeting different people", and I loved it, yeah (Nadia).

For these women, then, despite challenges earlier in their careers, their tourism careers were highly valued, and tourism came to be seen as a good career choice. Shariffa stated:

> It is a very good [career]. It was very good... as a first step for me. It was, really something good. It taught me a lot of things which, which I thought, "Ahhh, it's not important", but it is important, yeah.

Although the women were young and had a limited number of years of experience in the field, they seemed to have changed their views of tourism work, over a relatively short period of time.

6.2 Increased tourism development opportunities in Oman.

For the women in this study, tourism in Oman was seen as particularly important because of the role it played in terms of the country's history, culture, and development. As Khadija said,

> For me, that's the way I see it. But it depends on everybody and how they see it. But in general, I think it's a very big industry that you can be proud of, especially that Oman is one of the tourism places you can stay. It has some of our history, our culture. It's all about, you know, hospitality and tourism. I can say that. So, it's not like something you are trying to really to adapt to, it's in us [tourism and hospitality is a natural thing for Omanis]. It just really needs to be developed.

In addition, because the tourism industry is still growing in Oman, the women saw tourism employment as a growing opportunity. They were aware of the demand for tourism in Oman and expected new tourism development and projects to arise. As Fatima said,

> You see how, over the years, tourism has been such an important factor for this country - the number of guests, the number of businesses, the events and conferences that we are getting in Oman. And being in the hotel industry, we play a major role as well, like imagine if the airlines just dropped off the people. And then where would they stay? Where are they going to stay? There is competition-the hotels, the number of hotels that are going up. We were literally competing. So that, to me, is competition, and you know, I believe that tourism is the next source of income for this country.

Such vision of increased tourism development opportunities in Oman was also expressed by others:

> There are a lot of new projects, but they are all concentrated in Muscat [the country's capital], and Oman is huge. I mean there is so much to do, and there's a lot of work. I mean it's going to take years for it [to develop] (Aisha).

> Yeah yeah, with all this [increased tourism development] because of the government, and because of the projects that we are having, you know. It's a baby [Oman tourism industry]; it's growing (Salwa).

> Hmm, in future, let's say in five years from now, there will be a lot of demand, a lot of projects are coming up, hotels will be everywhere, every half an hour, there will be a hotel and there will be demand from tourists and from the local market (Nadia).

However, some of the women also thought that there was more that the government could do to improve tourism efforts and projects in Oman. As Zuwena urged, "Yes, there's a zillion ideas and I think they [the government] don't utilize the people who are in the industry for those. . . not only the ideas, but for training, for project development,... I really wish they would". Shariffa further emphasized this need for the government to work cooperatively with other industry players. She stated,

> Ahh, if you ask me, I think that the ministry of tourism... I think it recently started, maybe 3 to 4 years back, but still I feel that there are a lot of changes they need to do. The problem here is they [ministry of tourism] still, they are still thinking that they are [working alone]. They don't mix with other [industry players]. They don't mix with others, you know.

6.3 Increased opportunities for women.

Because of the increased tourism development opportunities in Oman, the women also saw tourism employment as an important opportunity for women in terms of increased jobs and demand for women. The women expressed the importance of having a job and bringing in income in order to support the family. This was also deemed necessarily because of the bad economy, as Zuwena commented on this by saying:

> At the moment is because ..., you know, the economy is really stale here. You know, life is tough... people are going to start working. If you look, I think, in the Middle East... if you look in the Emirates. I don't see Emirate women working, not even in a shop. We have women working at the gas station. That should tell you a lot [about the importance of jobs for women]. When the locals start coming out, even though we are Oman, doing Omanisation yes. But we have to work. We have no choice.

Other women also commented that people, and particularly women, now realize the importance of work despite the difficulty of finding appropriate jobs in Oman:

> But now people came to know... especially now. I mean it's quite difficult [to get a job] and some they came to know that, well, work is work. They need to work. Yeah, like before, especially in Omani culture, like they [women] feel shy to mix with the men and all these. So they like to only [mix with women]... It's like they only wanted to be either a teacher or a nurse, that's all...now thank God, everybody [I know thinks] "we have to work" (Munira).

> I think it's more of, ...people have moved on...like they accepted the development [tourism development]. They accepted it, and of course, secondary is the need for a job, and it doesn't matter which job is it, right now, as long there is income coming (Fatima).

As for the demand for women in the tourism industry, many talked about the importance of having women employees despite the negative attitudes. Women were seen to offer different skills from men, and the "feminine touch" was seen to be important. Women, it was argued, brought some unique skills to the tourism industry:

> Yes, it's because of the industry, you know. There are certain things where you need to have a female touch,... And there are so many opportunities. And I am not saying [this] just that they should be doing only guest relations or admin. I am like thinking of the front line - to have a female staff [person] really makes a difference (Fatima).

> I think it helps [the industry] because they [employers] do need this soft spot that women have. They do need it. And other than that, I mean for example in the banquet section...I mean ok

everything is set. This is how the table set up has to be. But a woman's taste is always better than a man's taste. So it will...it does affect in ways like that . . . in how things should go (Laila).

Further, because of the benefits that women could obtain through tourism work, this was seen to be a particularly good opportunity for women. Examples included:

> I think it's very good especially if they [women] work for companies that give programs that help them to travel or...like for me, they sent me to France to study, you know. They will get to see a lot more than maybe they would ever have had the opportunity [to see] (Aisha).

> In tourism, as I said, they [women] will benefit a lot. First of all, they will, build their ...they will gain experience. Second of all, the language, because the language here is difficult. So the language, it will be improved. Then it will [the problem of] mixing with people. It won't be there in their minds anymore [won't be an issue] because they will think it's, you know, [normal] (Shariffa).

> If you got this opportunity to work in a hotel, especially for those like they, they are still, they're new, they didn't work anywhere. So at least for them to start - even if you don't like the hotel industry, but just for a starting, like for one or two years, it's very good, yeah. You learn a lot of things from there yeah (Munira).

Some of the women said that they would definitely recommend and encourage their female relatives and friends to work in the tourism field:

> Hmmm, well, for me I like it a lot, and I recommend it because it's really good. I mean I enjoyed working in the tourism industry, and for me, I do encourage [others] yeah, I do encourage it (Khadija).

> For me, yes, I would encourage them. Yeah, even I would tell them to start from scratch, because there they will get, ...a lot of experience for themselves (Shariffa).

And Zuwena added:

> I encourage everybody, without fail. If I could make it mandatory, I would, honestly (Zuwena).

They were confident that there would be an increased demand for women to work in the tourism industry,

> There is a future [for women], and Omani ladies will be in the market, in this specific market [the tourism industry] (Nadia).

> Yes, there are a lot [of opportunities for women]. Like in the hotel itself, in the ... for example travel agencies, yeah, arranging tours, especially now in Oman. Yeah, tourism has [increased], so there are a lot of, opportunities. Lots of hotels are opening, yeah (Munira).

> In general, from now, yes, I think there are quite a lot of jobs for women out there [in the tourism industry], yeah (Khadija).

6.4 The need for better training and resources.

In order to encourage more women to work in the tourism industry, the women felt that there was a need for better training and resources for women to learn appropriate skills and to develop confidence. For example,

> Because in Oman, I mean unfortunately they might teach [theories of tourism employment] but I don't know, it's not serious [not the right kind of training]. I mean, we should take tourism as a serious sector, as a serious development. And whoever is coming out of these courses have to have the...have to have the confidence, the right attitude, the right person to be out there in hotels (Nadia).

> I think it's important, you know, to have the self-esteem, to build confidence. They [tourism colleges and training institutes] just tell them, "ok", it's in the book. You can just read it: the customer comes, the greeting has to be like this, when you answer the call and soon. That is it. But where I think, if they encourage them [the women] more, you know, to stand up in the class to start to talk about something - that is how they will build their confidence and self esteem (Sharrifa).

> I think it will be a good thing to...like before joining, like while you are studying, that they make a point of [teaching] communication skills [public speaking training] (Khadija).

> I mean if they have proper training, I think they really benefit. If you don't have proper training, I think, depending on the individual, you know a lot of times organizations also try to fool you - not fool you, but they say "ohh self development, self development". Well, not everybody can [develop on their own]. You can grow by yourself. There is no way you can stop yourself from growing, but in terms of improving one self, it's not always done on your own (Zuwena).

As for resources, the women expressed the need for employers to improve tourism job resources and use these resources to improve opportunities for women. In particular, Zuwena, a mother of 2 children, suggested using resources to provide suitable positions for women according to their life situation. She explained:

> A lot of the times I tell them [the employer] that one of our main problems, which they don't understand now, is HR (Human Resources). And HR plays a really big part in any industry. And they think it's just an administrative thing. But look, if you look at the positions that you have and you say, "Who do we need in this position? Do we need somebody who is not married, or who could get married and get pregnant and be sick you know? Or do we need somebody who is mature, who already has kids who are a bit older". I mean you have to also do that..., you know, that type of filtering, I feel they don't do that, so they fall into problems.

Consistent with this suggestion, Nadia talked about the importance of having jobs available for women that suited their particular needs, for example jobs with flexible hours, less weekend and holiday work and no late shifts:

> Like women who have young children between the ages, lets say zero to five or lets say four...maybe the hours should be more flexible, so we don't lose them...we don't lose them to another company. We need them there [in tourism employment]. They [the employers] have to take this seriously. And if they [women] leave, [they might get work] in banking, or elsewhere, maybe in oil and gas companies. But we need these women [in tourism work].

Zuwena made similar a suggestion by stating,

> I think they [employers] also could, for example, maybe re-adjust timing, which they used to do... You could do like a morning shift and have more women in the morning shift, and the men would have like a mid shift, where you can work, you know, like from 10 to 5 kinda of thing... You'll see the kids in the morning. You might miss them for lunch, but you are still there in the afternoon before they go to bed - that kind of thing, I think maybe that would help to increase the amount of women who would apply for jobs, knowing that they have...an option to choose some of these shifts.

In summary, this theme revealed the women's view of tourism as a growing field for employment for women. The women saw tourism employment as a growing opportunity because of the continuous growth of the tourism industry in Oman, and increased tourist demand and tourism development projects. The need for women to have a job due to the poor economy and the need to contribute to their family income made tourism work all the more attractive. Women were seen to have particular skills that were needed in the tourism field. However, emphasis was also placed on the need to help women develop their skills, competences and confidence. Also more resources were needed for the development of jobs that fit better with women's family responsibilities.

Theme 7: Implications for Social Change

Some of the comments made during the interviews indicated that the participants saw women's involvement in tourism work as having the potential to change attitudes to women in Oman society. In part this was due to their own successful career involvement and how evidence of female success might indirectly influence attitudes to women. A second more overt push for change related to the strategies that the women adopted to deliberately challenge dominant cultural attitudes and beliefs.

7.1 The importance of career success.

Some of the women in this study talked about their own accomplishments and achievements, while others talked about their goals and their determination to succeed. For all of them, career success was possible for women in the tourism industry, and success was deemed important because it was noticed by others and so might influence attitudes not only to them, but also to women in general. The following comments were made by women who had advanced to high-level positions in the industry, despite the male domination of these high positions:

> I [have] just recently been promoted into a guest relation's manager. I am currently working at a new hotel. I was actually there for the opening. I was one of the pre-opening team, and now I am working there (Fatima).

> Well, I started as an event coordinator but I didn't stay. I stayed only for a year and I switched to another job. But, comparing to my colleagues that were there, they got to another level now [they were promoted]. They were able to move on [advance in their career](Khadija).

Others were working on future success by trying different positions and seeking promotion through experience and hard work. For example,

> Well, I see myself like ok...I am working in customer service. I would like to see myself growing in the same department and I see myself as a manager or something (Khadjia).

> Yes, sales and marketing, but I mean my target, what I am thinking about is still to continue, yeah, with the hotel industry like for a couple of years - lets say, three or four more years, years but move in sales and marketing (Munira).

> Then I said "ok, this is enough for me". I think I gained enough experience through the travel agency, let me just move to, you know, airline, and see you know, what's the difference - how they work and all that (Shariffa).

No, I want to stay in this industry; I want to see how, how Oman is going towards the tourism industry. And what I am doing now is also in the tourism and it's helping me to see another, not only in the hotel, I mean I have seen the hotel of course (Nadia).

Ok, there, there are many females, Omani females [who are leaders] in the country. And I would like that so much. I would say I am not in that position where I am known and famous, you know, in society yet. But, you know, that is what I want (Salwa).

It was important, the women felt, for female employees to be "tough" and not to give up easily. This way, women's abilities and accomplishments would be recognized:

And there are so many women that have gone so far. If I look at them - how they got so far - it is because they were really tough and I am [tough too](Fatima).

Hmm, first of all, for Omani women, they shouldn't give up very easily. They should stay... not to stay and fight, but they should stay and improve themselves. Ahhh, you know, ask for training, do the job the right way. You might struggle and forget a few points. You are not going to [be perfect]. You have to show your bosses that you are doing the right job, and you will be promoted. They should... at the end of they day, they will be promoted (Nadia).

7.2 Challenging traditional attitudes.

The interviews also revealed that the women supported actions that deliberately challenged traditional ways of thinking. They thought that these actions would not only change Omani society, but that change was already occurring. Laila stated,

I mean if they [women] can implement their views and beliefs, then they can, for example, challenge society. Like I am a Muslim girl, I can do this, you know. There's nothing wrong with being, for example, at ten o'clock at the office you know, as long as I have a goal to reach. And it's challenging [societal attitudes]. And I have seen a lot of women who are doing this. They are challenging [attitudes], it [change] could happen.

The women also talked about the importance of tourism development in Oman, modernization, the changing economy, and the need for women in the tourism field. Collectively, these factors they felt, were already changing the old way of thinking and leading to more open mindedness. Fatima explained these changes this way,

Yeah, I believe that like for the old generation... The new generation, they have moved along with the development. They are much more open culturally. They are much more easy towards their daughters. So that's different. I mean, imagine the generations that are coming after us.

Aisha explained that increased education was also an indication of more open attitudes in society:

> Because women are now allowed to be educated, like in schools or something. And you have, I don't know how many thousands ever year being graduated from high school. And obviously they are going to be looking for employment. Either they go for further studies or they, you know, look for employment. It's [society] [becoming more] open (Aisha).

And Munira and Salwa related these changes to tourism work,

> Definitely. Because its [societal attitude] already started to change. Like people's [thinking] now and five years ago is different. So I feel like it's changing. Yes, like, for example, ...what I told you about...before you [wouldn't] find any Omani waitress in a hotel, but now you'll find them. Yes, so I feel it's...it will change...definitely, yes (Munira).

> You know because, ok, my argument is...I will give you an example, my mother. One of her concerns was who was going to marry a girl that works in a hotel, you know. And now she says, "There are people that are accepting female working [in a hotel] because it's [a hotel] just another building provided for work" (Salwa).

The women did caution that the old thinking still existed, but they felt it was less widespread than in previous years. Comments included,

> It [old thinking] still [exists]. Even if they [people with old thinking] don't bluntly say it ...it still exists (Laila).

> Yes, although we [society] are developing...[Negative attitudes] are not everywhere but they're still there (Khadija).

This theme revealed the women's perspectives on the changes that are occurring in terms of new attitudes towards women. Linked to the new view of tourism as a valuable industry that is strengthening the country's economy, new attitudes towards women working in this industry were becoming evident. Moreover this change was leading to new attitudes towards women in general. Despite the persistence of some traditional attitudes to women, the women felt that their work in the tourism industry was contributing to broader social change.

Summary

When looking at the seven themes discussed in this chapter, each theme represents an element in shaping the central underlying meaning of the women's experience in tourism employment. The first theme shows how the women's employment in the tourism industry often occurred by chance, due to the need for a job rather than a search for "career". At the beginning, many of the women lacked confidence in themselves and in their skills and abilities that were required for this kind of work. The second theme revealed the many challenges the women faced in their jobs because of negative attitudes of employers, family members, and society in general. These challenges tested the women's confidence and led to some conflicting feelings about their job. Family responsibilities and making time for family, husbands and children compounded these work-related challenges. However, the women in this study had all continued in tourism work and had found ways to deal with these challenges. This seemed to lead to growing confidence and a growing belief in the importance of tourism work for women. The benefits of tourism employment were seen to outweigh the challenges and negative attitudes that the women encountered. Many of the women seemed to gain strength, confidence, status and a sense of independence through their experiences in tourism work. Further, tourism work was seen to be of significant benefit, not only to them personally, but also in terms of broader social change. In particular, acceptance of women's tourism work, and successful careers for women in tourism, was seen to contribute to new attitudes towards women, and the potential for a new society.

Chapter 5: Discussion and Conclusion

The purpose of the discussion and conclusion chapter is to discuss the findings of the study and to provide insights and understanding based on the study. The first section of the chapter looks into the emergent themes, where the findings of the study are discussed. This is followed by a discussion of three broad issues, namely tourism work as exploitation, tourism work as empowerment and tourism as a source of social change, which connects the findings to the existing literature. The next section of the chapter looks into the study significance, followed by a discussion of the strengths and weaknesses of the research process as a whole. Possible future directions are discussed in terms of implications for tourism policy in Oman and for research on women's tourism employment. The chapter ends with my final thoughts and reflections on the study, the methods used, the findings, and the interpretations. Overall, the discussion and conclusion chapter provide a full discussion of the central issues surrounding the experiences of Muslim women employed in the tourism, and how these issues relate to the literature, to potential change and to future research.

Emergent Themes

In representing the experiences of Muslim women employed in the tourism industry, seven themes were developed from the analysis process. The seven themes were finding work in the tourism field, facing negative attitudes, challenges of tourism work, dealing with negative attitudes and challenges, importance of tourism work in the women's lives, an expanded vision of tourism work, and implications for social change. Collectively, these themes provide insight into the way Muslim women experience tourism employment and the meanings attached to this form of employment. These themes are important, since Muslim women's experiences in tourism employment have been largely overlooked. The seven themes reflect the phases that the women had to go through in their tourism employment experience in order to reach where they are today.

Theme 1, finding work in the tourism field, revealed that many of the women did not actively seek tourism employment and were unsure of their career choice at the beginning. Rather it was a series of sometimes unanticipated influences and outcomes that had led them to tourism employment. Discussion of how they obtained their first jobs revealed that jobs were scarce due to the high job competition and the preference, in many cases, for male employees. Tourism employment was thought of as a new opportunity for women but also one in which women encountered difficulties with access and with a lack of some of the attributes that seemed to be required. The women realized that they would need to learn and acquire these attributes in order to successfully work in the tourism industry, especially if they encountered negative attitudes and challenges along the way.

Indeed, the second theme revealed that women's employment in the tourism industry is still viewed negatively by many members of Omani society and that such perceptions continue to exist despite the increase of women in the workforce. That is, once women gained employment, they faced further difficulties. This theme revealed the pressures that women faced from society, family members and husbands, particularly with respect to concerns about women's reputation and honor if they worked in the tourism field. The women had to deal with these negative views if they wanted to continue in this line of work. Further, the women often struggled with their own conflicting feelings and concerns about tourism employment and their ability to perform their job successfully. Anticipation of these negative attitudes may have been linked to their uncertainty about tourism work.

In addition to the negative attitudes discussed above, the women faced other types of challenges in the work environment as discussed in theme 3. These challenges related to the work standards and expectations and were generally not anticipated ahead of time. Expectations that women were less capable than men to perform well in tourism work caused frustrations and constrained advancement to higher-level positions. Moreover, the challenges of tourism work, such as long hours, evening and weekend work, interfered with family time, family responsibilities, and traditional ideas about women's roles and the need to protect women's reputations. Women's tourism work was seen to challenge certain cultural values, and this was not necessarily alleviated by the involvement of expatriates in the tourism industry. Further, the low pay and low recognition compounded the stresses of tourism work for the women, sometimes leading to reduced job satisfaction. Because of these challenges, many of the women struggled to survive tourism employment and suffered self-doubts about continuing their employment in this field. One the other hand, the women interviewed for this study had continued their tourism work and had found ways to overcome some of these challenges.

Theme 4 revealed an important phase in the women's careers in which they found various ways to deal with the challenges they had experienced. Many of the strategies they used, such as "accepting and adapting to work expectations", were associated with the need to "prove themselves". They also, at times, sought to change the work situation. In terms of the challenge of dealing with work and family responsibilities, the women found different ways of dealing with child care issues. These strategies depended on the women's home situation, and included giving up on their career for a while, opting for a less demanding career, or working at home when possible. In terms of employers and societal attitudes, the women seemed to assume that they could not change such deeply embedded attitudes, so they opted to accept and conform rather than challenge. Despite this, many of the women did seek to change the attitudes of their family members and husbands. This may be because of the closeness of these relations and the need for their family members' approval. However, much depended on family members and husbands being open minded, understanding and liberal. This theme, then, revealed a mix of individual acceptance and adaption as well as some deliberate attempts to change attitudes.

The women in this study had accepted or overcome many of the challenges they faced in tourism work, allowing them to continue in this form of employment. This may help to explain their generally positive attitudes to working in the tourism field, and the benefits they saw from their employment, as revealed through theme 5. These benefits had not been apparent when they started along this career path, but later seemed to play an important role in terms of the importance of their tourism work. For the most part, they enjoyed their work and saw it as an important part of their lives. The women's determination and ability to adapt to the expectations of tourism work had led to new skills and had contributed to their career progress. The gains in strength, confidence, independence and status seemed to have led to a sense of empowerment and opened new doors. Moreover, they reported greater satisfaction in their work, compared to earlier in their career, and some talked of their work in tourism as a life-changing experience.

As seen earlier, the women's tourism employment was often entered into chance, due to the need for a job. However, over time and with increased confidence and empowerment, this form of work had become more than "just a job" for the women as revealed in theme 6. New and expanded meanings of tourism employment emerged, particularly with regard to the importance of tourism employment for women. The women in this study wanted to communicate this to other women, and encourage them to also seek tourism related careers. The women saw their involvement in tourism employment as being part of an important and growing economy in Oman. They also talked about the importance of better training and resources for women to enter and become successful in tourism employment. They felt that tourism work for women was important in terms of economic expansion, employment opportunities for women, and bringing benefits both to the tourism industry and to Omani women.

The expanded vision of tourism work was also evident in theme 7, which focused on the women's beliefs and hopes that increased female participation in tourism work could help to bring about fundamental change in Omani society. Tourism employment, they felt, could help to change traditional cultural norms and values, through women's career success . While the women in this study accepted and adapted to some traditional attitudes that they could not change, they did seek to change the attitudes of husbands and family members, and more significantly, they saw tourism employment as a means of changing the attitudes of women themselves. With the increased popularity of Oman as a tourist destination, the potential for increased female employment and for the social change benefits that might accrue were seen to be particularly important.

Tourism Work as Exploitation of Women

The exploitative nature of women's employment is a common theme in the tourism literature (e.g., Jordan, 1997; Sonmez, 2001). This study, too, provides some support for the idea of exploitation in terms of salary, working conditions and other challenges.

Low paid and unskilled work.

Much of the existing literature suggests that tourism employment is exploitation because it is low paid (Swain, 1995; Lucas, 2004; Enloe, 1989) and unskilled work (Jordan, 1997; Richter as cited in Sonmez, 2001). In addition, it is often women who largely fill these low skilled and low paid jobs because such jobs are accessible to women who may lack formal education. However, when looking at the findings of this study, the issue of exploitation was not straightforward for these Omani women. The women talked about general job access difficulties and about the lack of employment opportunities for women in Oman. Against this background, they felt that the increased availability of tourism work for them had provided valued opportunities for employment, despite the low salary and low skilled work. This reflects Winckler's (2007) suggestion that the development of the tourism industry in Oman has provided new work opportunities, particularly for women. Additional support comes from a Gulf News report that suggested that Omani nationals were open to accepting jobs at modest salaries (as cited in Winckler, 2007). With the tourism industry being fairly new, and with the increased opportunities for tourism and hospitality education in Oman, this study indicated that this form of work was attractive to women, particularly to women from rural areas where job opportunities are scarce and limited. This might explain why these women did not talk about their work as a form of exploitation, although they received low pay and were doing low skilled work.

Limited career advancement.

Another aspect of the exploitation of women, as reported in the literature, is the lack of opportunities for women to advance in tourism work, to be promoted to better positions and to improve their career. This is because there is often a preference for men employees in higher paid and higher level positions. This seems to be the case in Oman, as reported by the women in this study and in previous research by Kinnaird et al. (1994), Enloe (1989), and Swain (1993, 1995). In addition, this study found that women needed to work particularly hard in order to prove themselves for promotions. This is similar to Jordan (1997) and Richter's (as cited in Sonmez, 2001) suggestions that women have less access to managerial positions. In fact, progress for women in Islamic cultures may be more difficult than in other cultures. This is because of the negative attitudes towards female employment, and the strongly rooted belief that women are less skilled than men, and that they are less committed to their work because of their primary roles as mothers and wives.

Working hours.

The problem of long working hours, "unsocial" hours, evenings, weekends and unpredictable work hours, can also be seen as a form of exploitation of women in the tourism industry. This issue was raised by Riley et al (2002) who suggested that many tourism employees work unsocial hours and have less social time outside of work. In addition, Riley et al (2002) also suggested that the constant fluctuations of consumer demand in tourism require employees to work unpredictable hours. The issue of working hours was a particularly difficult issue for the women in this study because of their socially assumed responsibilities for home, family and children. Again, this may be particularly problematic for women in Muslim societies because of traditional attitudes about women and women's roles (Doumato and Posusney, 2003).

The issue of working hours was also evident in the employers' negative attitudes towards married women and women with children and the expectation that they would be less committed to their jobs. This can be seen as a form of exploitation of women, placing a major burden on these women who attempt to work, while at the same time, placing a major expectation on women to marry and produce. For women, this leads to difficulty in balancing family responsibilities and work requirements, and some women give up on their tourism employment because of the difficult working hours. This confirms Shaben et al.'s (1995) point that Muslim women withdraw early from the labor force due to the pressure of marriage and child bearing. In addition, husbands may make it difficult for women to conform to required working hours, as they may expect their wives to put their home, families and children first. Evening and weekend hours were a particularly difficult issue for the Omani women in this study because of having less social time with their family and husbands. Thus, expected working hours sometimes led to problems and conflicts at home.

Societal and cultural barriers.

Also related to the issue of women's roles in Muslim societies are cultural attitudes towards Muslim women's employment in the tourism industry. First, the idea of work is not perceived to be part of a Muslim woman's role. As Moghadam (2003) has pointed out, there is a social stigma in Muslim societies attached to women who participate in work. Indeed, in some Muslim societies, there are debates over whether women should be allowed to work at all (Keddie, 1991).

A second issue is that tourism work is thought to be particularly inappropriate for women because it involves mixing with men and coming into contact with men and strangers from other cultures. As Sonmez (2001) points out, it is deemed inappropriate and strongly objectionable in Islamic cultures for different sexes to mix. Further, Shaban et al's (1995) research showed that Muslim families have a cultural preference for women to work only in employment sectors deemed to be appropriate. Although there is increased encouragement from the government for women in Oman to work in the tourism industry (Winckler, 2007), this study has shown that cultural and societal attitudes seem to contradict this government initiative. Thus, this raises some important policy questions.

Many of the negative attitudes discussed above are also related to the idea of family honor and reputation. That is, the idea that men (e.g., husbands and fathers) need to control women's work in order to maintain their family's honor and reputation, and to avoid consequences of shame (Moghadam, 2003; Riphenburg, 1998). This issue arose in the present study, consistent with the suggestions that the status of women in the Omani society is largely influenced by their family members and husbands (Gray & Finely-Hervey, 2005; Riphenburg, 1998). Besides dealing with the attitudes of husbands and family members, this study showed that women also face cultural discrimination from expatriates when it comes to job competition and Omani cultural values. Again, this is consistent with previous research from Saudi Arabia (Sadi & Henderson, 2005) that suggested that hiring expatriates often involves controversy and negative consequences for domestic job seekers.

Overall, this study and previous research suggests that women's employment in tourism in Oman can be seen as a form of exploitation in a number of ways such as the low pay, unskilled work, lack of progress, and inappropriate working hours. Further, these forms of exploitation are compounded by other difficulties that women face with regards to societal and cultural attitudes both towards women's work in general, and towards tourism work in particular. Yet, an interesting aspect that emerged from the study is that most of the women did not seem to feel that they were being exploited. They certainly did recognize the problems and challenges surrounding tourism employment. In some instances, they tried to conform to social expectation. At the same time, they found various ways to deal with other challenges such as seeking to change attitudes of family members and husbands. More importantly, once they adapted to, accepted, or sought to change some of these challenges, the women seemed to start to see tourism work as an "opportunity" and as "progress" rather than as "exploitation". Therefore, the idea of exploitation, with regard to the women interviewed in this study, was complex and multi-layered. Clearly, the situation is not a simple case of exploitation, but a complex mix of challenges, difficulties, and overcoming difficulties in order to benefit from the opportunities that this form of work was seen to offer.

Tourism Work as Empowerment for Women

Despite some evidence of exploitation, the women in this study seemed to have a different perspective on their work. These women had continued with their tourism employment and survived or overcome many of the obstacles that challenged their career success. Clearly, they valued their employment. Not only did they associate tourism work with a number of benefits, their comments suggested that their work could be seen as a form of empowerment. This related to their positive experiences, and how these experiences influenced their feelings about themselves.

Fun and enjoyment.

All of the women talked about enjoying aspects of their work, despite the difficulties. This is consistent with Purcell's (1997) work that suggested that tourism employment is seen as more "fun" compared to other types of work. In this study, the women's enjoyment of tourism work came largely from the opportunities it offered in terms of new experiences, learning about different cultures and meeting different people. This included the opportunity to meet and interact with tourists, clients and other people. Being comfortable with these social interactions seemed to lead to greater satisfaction with and commitment to their tourism work and supports. Riley et al (2002) suggested that the nature of tourism employment, which includes meeting people, may act as an incentive to women and counteract some of the negative aspects of tourism work.

Learning new skills.

Meeting different people and being exposed to new situations also provided an opportunity for the women to learn new skills, such as learning how to deal with different types of people. They also learned to be comfortable in new situations, which they had not experienced before. These new skills, associated with customer service, presentations, leadership, dealing with different people and situations, writing, and time management etc., seemed to give the women strength and more confidence in themselves. In addition, their growing competencies helped them with their future career progress and made promotions more possible. Although the women felt that certain "personalities" were required for work in tourism, as noted earlier, most of the skills that the women gained were learned on the job and through the various training opportunities that were offered in their work place. This is consistent with Riley et al's (2002) observation that the skills required for tourism employment can easily be learned on the job. Further, this study showed that these skills can easily be transferred to different job opportunities and to higher-level positions in the tourism field.

Gaining confidence, independence, and status.

With the increase in confidence, the women seemed to develop a growing sense of independence as well. This was due to various factors such as the opportunity to work, to gain skills, and to be able to deal with various challenges on their own. This is similar to Gentry's (2007) study on Belizean women and tourism work, where Belizean women also cited increased self-confidence and independence as a result of their experience in tourism employment. Many of the Belizean women were able to find employment in tourism work and open their own businesses, thus reducing their reliance on men for financial security. Although the cultures of Oman and Belize are quite different when it comes to religion and culture, nevertheless, women in Oman and Belize share similar expectations about gender roles responsibilities for their homes and families. Despite the different cultures, the experiences of these two groups of women seem to be similar.

The concept of independence for women contradicts Swain's (1995) model of the "male breadwinner/female dependence relations in the home". However, both this study and Gentry's study suggest that tourism provides opportunities for women to have independent incomes and to provide needed income to support their families. Thus, it weakens rather than strengthens the idea of the male breadwinner. Although the domination of men in Islamic societies still exists, tourism work can reduce women's financial reliance on men. This supports Sonmez's (2001) vision for Middle Eastern women to take advantage of tourism wage-earning opportunities in order to gain independence similar to women in other parts of the world.

Besides financial independence, the study also showed that the gained independence in terms of decision-making and dealing with the various difficulties they faced. The nature of tourism work seemed to offer unique situations in terms of the various challenges and obstacles faced and the need to make important decisions about how to deal with these situations. In addition, the women benefitted from a growing sense of status. The tourism industry in Oman is still developing and is seen to be making an important economic contribution to the country. Thus, the women felt that their work in tourism employment was playing a major role in the country's development. They also felt proud to be part of the tourism industry despite the negative societal attitudes that are held towards this form of work. In addition, through their tourism work, they felt they were promoting their country and representing the country's culture and hospitality. This, they felt, earned them respect from others. This aspect of status and respect has not been discussed in previous literature and so provides a new perspective on women's tourism employment. A considerable number of authors have discussed Muslim women's status (e.g. Baden, 1992; Gray & Finely-Hervey, 2005; Moghadam, 2003; Sonmez, 2001). However, the potential to gain status from tourism employment, and for Muslim women to feel that they play an important role in their society because of their work in this industry, has not been discussed.

Empowerment.

Overall, the concepts discussed above, including fun and enjoyment, learning new skills, and gaining confidence, independence and status, suggest the broader idea of empowerment. Given the benefits that the women gained during their career, it is perhaps not surprising that they thought of their career as providing a life changing experience. They also believed that tourism employment would benefit other women as well. This sense of personal change as well as advocating tourism work for other women is consistent with Hutchison and McGill's (1992) definition of empowerment as:

> An interactive process through which people experience personal and social change, enabling them to take action to achieve influence over the organizations and institutions which affect their lives and the communities in which they live
>
> (p.34)

In this study, the women faced challenges and negative attitudes, but were able to overcome these difficulties and to be successful in their careers. This is consistent with Harris and Wilson's (2007) suggestion that "overcoming constraints and limitations can lead to feelings of achievement and an increased feeling of power" (p. 238). In addition, the ability for the women to find different ways of dealing with the challenges they faced can also be seen as a form of empowerment through independent decision-making. This also fits with Rehman, Junankar and Mallik's (2009) definition of the empowerment of women:

> An empowered woman is confidant in her ability; she is capable of leading her life independently; she is socially as well as economically independent; she is opinionated, enlightened and has freedom from all sorts of domination; and finally she is someone who is capable of standing for her own rights (p. 290)

Thus, this study reveals some of the complexities of women's tourism employment. While tourism employment as exploitation has been a feature of previous literature, the contradictory idea of empowerment also emerged from this study, suggesting positive as well as negative effects of tourism employment on women's lives.

Tourism as a Source of Social Change

Related to the women experiencing personal change in their lives through tourism employment, the idea of tourism employment as a source of social change also emerged as a possibility. Indeed the women in the study talked about various ways in which female employment in the tourism industry in Oman could potentially contribute to social change and create a "new society".

The image of the tourism industry.

This study, as well as previous reports on tourism (e.g., Inskeep, 1994) has indicated the image of tourism and tourism employment in Oman is tarnished by various cultural, religious and social concerns. The fear seems to be that the tourism industry, which is still fairly new in Oman, may diminish the saliency of traditional cultural and religious norms. This supports Burns and Cooper's (1997) argument that there is a conflict between modern western tourism and Islamic cultures in that tourism is seen to dilute Islamic culture. Thus, as Baum and Conlin (1997) point out, Muslim societies tend to take a cautious view of tourism and seek to protect the community and cultural values from the western influence of incoming modern tourism.

However, the women in this study had, and also advocated for, a positive image of the tourism industry. This was evident through their emphasis on the economic significance of the tourism industry through increased tourist demand and tourism development projects. In addition, the women talked about the role of the tourism industry in providing increased employment opportunities for the local population, including women.

Tourism as an appropriate employment for women.

The women interviewed were very keen to promote tourism as an appropriate form of employment for women. Tourism employment, they argued, could provide women with needed income to support their families, and this was see as important because of the poor economy. The women's advocacy was also evident through their deliberate attempts to change the attitudes of their family members and husbands to make them more accepting of tourism work for women. This advocacy on the part of female tourism workers is an important finding, which has not been addressed in previous tourism literature.

Indeed, whether or not it is due to women's advocacy, there does seem to be a gradual change in societal attitudes to tourism and to women's employment in this industry. This probably relates to economic concerns, low oil revenues and awareness of the economic potential of tourism development (Winckler, 2007). While the evidence of attitudes change to date is limited, Doumato and Posusney's (2003) discussion of globalization effects does suggests that these effects are linked to the evolving role of women in the Middle East. They claim that new values are emerging that incorporate many western perspectives, including employment opportunities for women. Thus this suggests that societal values are gradually being transformed.

Desire to change attitudes to women in general.

Besides the women's attempts to advocate for tourism employment for women, the study also revealed the women's desire to see new societal and cultural attitudes towards women in general. One aspect of this was the desire for new attitudes to women's employment. They also saw a need for new attitudes about women's abilities and competencies as employees with the potential for promotion and career success. Their own experiences proved that women could find ways to deal with the challenges of the work place and could find ways to balance work and home responsibilities. However, new cultural attitudes related to gender, gender roles and assumed responsibilities were needed, they felt, in Omani society in general.

It was evident from the study that the women were very conscious of wanting to make or encourage these changes, and they argued for some specific actions to accomplish this. For example, they felt strongly that there was a need for improved training and resources for women to work in the tourism field and for making tourism employment more accessible for women. They were also deliberate in making changes in their own lives by seeking to change attitudes towards their tourism work by working hard and aiming for enhanced career progress. In addition, the women were also intentionally encouraging other women to work in the tourism field because of the possible benefits for themselves, for the tourism field, and for society in general. They felt that women's unique "feminine" skills should be recognized, making this form of employment more acceptable and more attractive to women. These deliberate attempts for change support Phillimore's (2002) suggestion that women should be seen as agents, making deliberate choices about tourism employment rather than succumbing to gender and employment discrimination. They also relate to Gray and Finely-Hervey's (2005) study of women and entrepreneurship in Morocco, where Moroccan women were deliberately bypassing many rules and regulation regarding women's employment by pursuing entrepreneurship opportunities. Thus, it is evident that the women in this study did not only see tourism employment as being good for themselves, but also as potentially good for other women and for society as a whole, leading to more openness and acceptance of Omani women's evolving roles.

Resistance to cultural attitudes.

Taken as a whole, the women's perspectives, comments, hopes, behaviors and actions can be seen as a form of "resistance" against traditional cultural norms, beliefs and ideologies about women in the Oman society. According to Shaw (2001),

> Resistance is conceptualized as acts that challenge the structured power relations of class, race, disability, ethnicity, gender, sexual orientation, or other forms of societal stratifications. It is oppressed or disadvantaged groups or individuals, who are acting to change power relations and gain personal or collective empowerment, who are seen to exemplify resistance (p.188)

In this study, the women's deliberate advocacy for change in terms of their personal lives, other women's lives, changes in the tourism industry, and changes in cultural attitudes towards women in general can be seen as forms of intentional resistance (Shaw, 2001). The women's ability and motivation to resist traditional dominant views of women may have been facilitated through the empowerment they gained from tourism employment. Thus, they were using tourism employment as a form of resistance, not only for individual empowerment but also for a broader societal change. Tourism may have provided one of the few avenues available for women to challenge the strong cultural and religious norms of the country. Both Shaw (2001) and Wearing (as cited in Harris and

Wilson, 2007) have argued that women can use leisure as a means to challenge their own lack of power or dissatisfaction with the dominant discourse. In this study, though, it was tourism employment, which provided them with a "flexible and optimistic situation grounded in their everyday experiences" (Henderson & Hickerson, 2007, p. 598), which seemed to enable acts of resistance.

The idea of tourism employment as a site for women's resistance can be seen as a new way of understanding the potential role of tourism employment for women in Muslim societies. While the notion of leisure as a site for women's resistance has been addressed in previous literature (Henderson & Hickerson, 2007; Parry, 2005; Raisborough & Bhatti, 2007; Shaw, 2001), it is relatively new in the tourism literature, and requires further exploration.

Study Significance

Much of the past literature on tourism employment has concentrated on the exploitation of employees, particularly women. Although this study had found some support for the notion of exploitation with the barriers that Muslim women face because of cultural and religious attitudes, the study also revealed many benefits of tourism employment, and that these benefits seemed to outweigh the challenges. Hence, the idea of exploitation can not be seen as a general rule when it comes to understanding the role of tourism employment for women. More significantly, tourism employment was also shown to be a form of empowerment for women, which was facilitated through the various benefits that were gained and the life changes experienced. And lastly, the study revealed that tourism employment can also be a site for women's resistance, particularly for Muslim women seeking to change attitudes towards women, and to create a new society. Although a few of the studies that have been done on tourism employment for Muslim women have provided some insight on the possible benefits and opportunities of tourism employment, this study provided an in-depth understanding of the experiences of a select group of Muslim women employed in the tourism industry.

This study is also important in that it reveals the complicated issues surrounding the influence of religion and culture. These issues have been discussed previously by Nga-Longvna (as cited in Sonmez, 2001 p.127), who says that there is a "general tendency to assess women's opportunities and constraints in terms of what the Quran and Islamic tradition dictate, not in terms of secular and more immediate concerns they may share with the rest of society". This study has looked at the benefits and constraints in terms of women's lives and women's concerns. That is, it has provided direct insight into the difficulties that Muslim women encounter in terms of cultural and religion, and shows how this provides an understanding of the ability of Muslim women to find different ways to cope, overcome and prevail against these difficulties. Further, the study has shown the considerable benefits that the women gained from their tourism employment, thus displaying the importance of tourism employment on the women's lives.

The earlier literature review revealed that stereotypes still exist about Muslim women who are characterized as being weak, oppressed (Gray & Finely-Hervey, 2005) and/or submissive (Sonmez, 2001). This study presents a different image of Muslim women, and suggests that tourism work plays a role in assisting women to overcome traditional stereotypes. It shows that some women do actively resist religious and cultural constraints, and that their work in tourism is an important part of this resistance, with the potential for individual empowerment as well as for possible social change.

As Seiklay (1994) has pointed out, Muslim women's experiences vary from country to country. In the case of Oman, there is a moderate climate of tolerance towards the empowerment of women. This, however, does not mean that cultural and religious constraints have disappeared. Rather, we see that women do face constraints, but that some of them are able to challenge these constraints, for example through their employment in tourism.

Despite Alvi's (2005) concern that the Middle East region has failed to empower women, this study shows there is hope for enhanced power for Muslim women. In particular, industries such as tourism can help facilitate that empowerment as revealed through the data. The study suggests that changes, such as tourism development, can potentially have a major affect on society in general as well as on individual women. Although Sonmez (2001) did point out that the numbers of women employed in the Middle East are low in comparison to developed countries, the findings of the study are encouraging, and increased employment opportunities may develop and may facilitate greater gender equality and societal development in the future.

The study also helps to enhance understanding of the roles of women in different cultural and societal settings. Thus, it contributes to cross-cultural understanding. It is hoped that this research will contribute to knowledge of the issues surrounding the lives of Muslim women in the Middle East. More specifically, it is also hoped that this research provides a better understanding of Modern Muslim women working in the tourism industry. Although the status of women in Oman is better compared to some other Muslim countries, the study provides an insight into the challenges they face in their daily lives in this Muslim society. Overall, the study provides an understanding of the experiences and meanings of tourism employment for Muslim women in Oman, including the positive and negative aspects of this form of employment. Women in other Middle Eastern countries may also experience some of these challenges and benefits.

Strength and Weaknesses

The following discussion reflects on the research process used in this study in terms of the strengths and weaknesses:

Social constructionism.

The use of social constructionsim was an important aspect of this study, providing a framework that focused on understanding meanings, perspectives and experiences, and their relationship to the social construction of reality. This framework directed attention to the social context of the participants' lives and the various cultural and religious norms imposed on them. For example, the negative attitudes and assumed roles that the women discussed in this study revealed the various cultural and religious norms that Muslim women encountered in their daily lives and how these norms conflicted with their choice to work. The framework also suggested the need to consider how work situation can be experienced differently by different people, under different circumstances, in different environments, and in different cultures. For example, the work conditions that were revealed in the study could be seen as exploitation by some women in some environments. However, women in this study focused more on the benefits of tourism employment, and the challenges of tourism employment were less transparent.

Furthermore, the focus on agency within social constructionism suggests that people can respond in a variety of ways to negative situations, for example difficult work conditions, families and husbands concerns of work type, etc., by adapting to expectations, changing some circumstances or challenging them. In the case of the women in this study, they adopted all three ways of dealing with the negative attitudes and challenges of tourism work. Lastly, the use of social constructionism provided a framework for exploring how everyday actions can be a form of resistance, not only with regard to personal situations or the lack of personal power, but also resistance against broader cultural beliefs and ideologies. For example, the women's perspectives, comments, hopes, behaviors and deliberate actions through tourism employment revealed their resistance to the negative attitudes that the women faced at the beginning of their career, as well as their desire for social change for themselves, for other women, and for society as a whole.

Grounded theory.

The use of grounded theory was also an important component of this study. The grounded theory approach was consistent with the initial research questions and with the qualitative/interpretive approach used in this study. It allowed me to use my background as an Omani, a Muslim, and a tourism professional in interpreting the data while being sensitive to cultural and religious issues. While developing a fully integrated "grounded theory" was not the intention of the study, the approach was helpful in terms of the development of themes that were grounded in the data and developing the beginning of a theory of Muslim women's experiences in the tourism industry. In particular, the use of the grounded theory approach for the analysis of the data was helpful and important in assigning codes and categories to the data in order to develop the themes and thematic properties. The grounded theory approach also allowed me to explore the relationships between themes during the analysis process. For example, the analysis helped me to see the developed themes as phases that the women had to go through in order to develop the perspectives that they currently had of tourism employment. And lastly, the need to revisit the literature during and after the analysis was helpful in ensuring the accuracy and relevance of the developed themes and for theoretical sensitivity. The use of memo writing was also helpful in terms of keeping track of thoughts, ideas and questions while interpreting the data. A considerable amount of time was required to analyze the data because of the various coding stages that are required for grounded theory. However, this was important in order to ensure all information was explored and extracted from the data. Hence, grounded theory allowed me to present the data in a meaningful way and to provide new knowledge.

The interviews.

The use of interviews was appropriate for understanding experiences and meanings of the women employed in the tourism industry. In particular, semi-structured interviews allowed for open discussion, while also ensuring that potentially important issues assigned in the interview guide were covered in all interviews. For example, the question about completed formal tourism and hospitality education was open-ended, allowing for informal discussion of what they liked about their educational experience and whether it was useful for their tourism employment. An interesting aspect that emerged from the semi-structured interviews was that it also allowed new and unexpected issues to emerge that were not originally assigned to the interview guide. For example, the idea around women providing a unique "feminine touch" and the issue around competition with expatriates were new and unexpected issues raised during the interviews. With the emergence of new ideas and concepts, I could then probe further on these issues in order to seek clarification and elaboration in upcoming interviews.

As for using English in the interviews, there did not seem to be any problems from this in terms of understanding the questions asked or the women's ability to express their feelings and opinions in English. This is because speaking English is quite common and often preferred among young people in Oman. Also, English is a formal subject in Oman's education system, and speaking and writing in English is required in order to work in the tourism industry in Oman. In addition, using English in the interviews required no translation. This made it easier to transcribe and analyze the interviews.

However, in order to make sure that all of the quotations were readable and understandable, clarification of language use in some of the quotes was needed.

Member checks.

The use of member checks played a role in ensuring the accuracy of the interpretation of the data in representing the women's real meanings and experiences. The women were all interested in receiving a summary report on the results of the study. However, only four of the women responded to the summary reports by providing feedback and comments. In addition, their feedback was very brief and limited. The length of time that it took to transcribe and analyze the data may explain the limited replies that were received for the summary reports, where some of the women may have lost interest in the study. Nevertheless, the received feedback was positive in terms of agreement with the main conclusions of the study and evident of continued enthusiasm about taking part in the study. This provided me with increased confidence in the results of my study.

Sample.

The use of convenience sampling made it possible for me to recruit participants through the use of friends and previous colleagues in Oman. In addition, the use of snowball sampling was beneficial in meeting additional participants through these contacts. Both sampling techniques made the recruitment process easier and all of the interviews were conducted within a two-month period. However, there were some contacts made with potential participants who were not interviewed. This was mostly due to the difficulty of setting up an interview as a result of their busy schedules. Some other women did not agree to be interviewed for personal reasons. Among the women who did participate, all were very keen and excited to be part of the study. They seemed to be open and comfortable discussing all of the issues and having their interviews tape-recorded.

Lastly, it should be noted that the women in this study seemed to be exceptional in a number of ways. For example, they had all been able to manage the various challenges and attitudes that they encountered in their tourism work. In addition, the women seemed to be highly competent and were committed to progressing in their tourism career. Some had been promoted to higher-level positions and others had tried different tourism work positions. Although I was not able to interview women who had dropped out of tourism employment, the women in this study did talk about many other women who had resigned because of not being able to handle the challenges and negative attitudes. This suggests that women who dropped out of tourism employment may have had different experiences or responded differently to these experiences. And lastly, the women who participated in my study were employed in relatively specific type of tourism work, where they dealt primarily with "high end" tourists. This may have led to additional challenges in terms of dealing with difficult customers and meeting customer service expectations.

Overall, the women involved in this study may have represented an emerging group of modern women who are resisting and reconstructing their own strong views and beliefs, as other women do in other parts of the world.

Future Directions for Tourism and Research in Oman

The study provides important information that has implications for the development and practice of Oman's tourism policy. It also raises additional questions related to women's employment in the tourism field. Although the government of Oman has approached tourism development carefully in order to protect the cultural values and the environment, the findings of the study suggest that the government did not carefully assess the possible conflicts that may arise towards tourism employment because of cultural and religious beliefs, and attitudes towards women working. A public education campaign about tourism employment would be helpful to increase awareness among the women and their families about tourism work and the opportunities available. There is also a need to provide better training and resources for women in order to make this form of work more accessible for women and to help build their skills and competencies through appropriate training.

When it comes to research surrounding tourism employment, many authors focus on the negative aspects of tourism, such as the seasonality of tourism work (Faulkenberry, Coggeshal, Backman & Backman, 2000; Gmelch, 2004), the low pay and low skills required, the limited chances for advancement (Chant, 1997; Pattulo, 1996), and the gendered nature of tourism employment (Gentry, 2007). While all of these issues are important, some attention also needs to be given to the potential for positive aspects, particularly for women from certain cultures such as Muslim societies. In addition, more studies need to be done on the work conditions in different cultural contexts and to examine in more depth the influence of different social, political, religious and economic settings. Only a few studies have looked at these issues to date. This includes Gentry's (2007) report on both opportunities and impediments facing female Belizean tourism workers. Also Ghodsee (2003) found that tourism employment in Post-Socialist Bulgaria was considered to have good working conditions. These studies provide support for the notion that tourism employment conditions and demands may vary depending on the country's culture and work setting.

In terms of future research with Muslim women, there are a variety of studies that could be done to enhance understanding and to develop my theory further. Within Oman, for example, tourism employment is being promoted throughout the country. However, the experiences of women from different parts of Oman may vary. In comparison to Muscat (the capital of Oman, where interviews for this study were held), women from the rural and interior areas of Oman face greater restrictions and constraints due to religious and cultural influences. Therefore, research is needed to understand the different ways in which tourism employment may affect women from these areas. Also, as I was not able to interview women in Oman who may have had a more negative experience or dropped out of tourism employment, it would be interesting and important to talk to these women as well, in order to compare their experiences with the women in this study. Furthermore, studying the perspectives of Omani men may be helpful in terms of identifying the commonalities and differences with regard to the experiences of men and women employed in the tourism industry. Lastly, in order to increase further cross-cultural understanding and to identify the commonalities and differences among the world's women, further studies need to be conducted in other Muslim countries as well as in developed and developing countries to better understand the ways in which tourism employment is related to, or affected by, modernization and globalization.

Final Thoughts

My journey as a Muslim woman, who is passionate about the tourism industry still continues. I believe that my study has provided an understanding of the experiences and meanings of tourism employment for a group of Muslim women. These women are prospering and living modern lives, primarily due to their employment in the tourism industry. Throughout this journey, I have enjoyed pursuing this research and talking to the different women that I have interviewed as I believe I share a common interest with them.

Through my research, I hope to be able to open more doors for other women to pursue research in this area since more research is required. I also hope, with the help of the women that I have interviewed, to encourage more women to be involved in tourism employment and to gain many of the benefits and opportunities that are possible through this form of employment. Overall, my journey continues with the hope of increasing awareness of the opportunities associated with tourism employment for women.

References

Abdul-Ghani, M. (2006). Hospitality and tourism education in the making: The case of the Sultanate of Oman. *Journal of Teaching in Travel and Tourism.* 6 (2), 71-87.

Al Mahadin, S. & Burns, P. (2007). Visitors, visions and veils: The portrayal of the Arab world in tourism advertising. In Daher, R. (Eds.), *Tourism in the Middle East: Continuity, change and transformation* (pp.137-160). Clevedon: Channel View publications.

Al-Jabi, R. (2003). The effects of globalization on Arab women workers. *Journal of Women Studies and Research in Iran and Muslim Countries*, 6 (11), 27-53.

Alvi, H. (2005). The human rights of women and social transformation in the Arab Middle East. *Middle East Review of International Affairs*, 9 (2), 142-160.

Arnold, S. (1997). Gulf Tourism. *The Middle East*, 267, 18-21.

Aziz, H. (2001). The journey: An overview of tourism and travel in the Arab/Islamic context. In Harrison, D. (Eds.), *Tourism and the less developed world: Issues and case studies* (pp.151-159). Oxon, UK: CABI publishing.

Baden, S. (1992). The position of women in Islamic countries: Possibilities, constraints and strategies for change. *Bridge (Development-Gender)-Institute of Development Studies*, 4, 1-41.

Baum, T. & Conlin, M. (1997). Brunei Darussalam: Sustainable tourism development within an Islamic cultural ethos. In Go, F. & Jenkins, C. (Eds.), *Tourism and economic development in Asia and Australasia* (pp.91-102). London, UK: Pinter.

Blumer, H. (1969). *Symbolic interactionism: Perspective and method.* Englewood Cliffs, New Jersey: Prentice Hall.

Bolles, A. (1997). Women as a category of analysis in scholarship on tourism: Jamaican women and tourism employment. In Chambers, E. (Eds.), *Tourism and culture-An applied perspective* (pp.77-92). Albany: State university of New York Press.

Burns, P. (1993). Sustaining tourism employment. *Journal of Sustainable Tourism*, 1 (2), 81-97.

Burns, P. & Cooper, C. (1997). Yemen: Tourism and a tribal-Marxist dichotomy. *Tourism Management*, 18 (8), 555-563.

Chant, S. (1997). Gender and tourism employment in Mexico and the Philippines. In Sinclair, M. T. (Eds.), *Gender, work and tourism* (pp.119-178). London: Routledge.

Charmaz, K. (2006). *Constructing grounded theory: A practical guide through qualitative analysis.* Thousands Oaks, CA: Sage publications.

Choufany, H. & Younes, E. (2005). Oman-Today's spotlight, tomorrow's destination. *HVS International London* .June, 1-14.

Creswell, J. (2003). *Research design: Qualitative, quantitative and mixed methods approaches* (2nd ed.). Thousand Oaks: Sage publications.

Cukier, J. (2002). Tourism employment issues in developing countries: Examples from Indonesia. In Sharpley, R. & Telfer, D. (Eds.), *Tourism and development: Concepts and Issues* (pp.165-201). Clevedon, UK: Channel View publications.

Daly, K. J. (2007). *Qualitative methods for family studies and human development.* Thousands Oaks, CA: Sage publications.

Din, K.H. (1989). Islam and tourism: Patterns, issues and options. *Annals of Tourism Research*, 16, 542-563.

Doumato, E. & Posusney, M. (2003). *Women and globalization in the Arab Middle East: Gender, economy and society.* Boulder, Colorado: Lynne Rienner Publishers.

Enloe, C. (1989). *Bananas, beaches and bases: Making feminist sense of international politics.* Berkeley: University of California Press.

Faulkenberry, L. J., Coggeshall, J., Backman, K. & Backman, S. (2000) A culture of servitude: The impact of tourism and development on South Carolina's coast. *Human Organization,* 59 (1), 86-95.

Finn, M., Elliott-White, M. & Walton, M. (2000). *Tourism and leisure research methods: Data collection, analysis and interpretation.* Harlow: Longman.

Fordyce, J., Rhadi, L., Maurice, D., Van Arsdol, Jr. & Deming, M. (1985). The changing roles of Arab women in Bahrain. In Nugent, J. & Thomas, T. (Eds.), *Bahrain and the Gulf: Past perspectives and alternative futures* (pp.56-72). Kent: Croom Helm Ltd.

Gentry, K. (2007). Belizean women and tourism work: Opportunity or impediment? *Annals of Tourism Research, 34 (2), 477-496.*

Ghodsee, K. (2003). State support in the market: Women and tourism employment in post-socialist Bulgaria. *International Journal of Politics, Culture and Society,* 16 (3), 465-482.

Glasse, C. (1989). *The concise encyclopedia of Islam.* San Francisco: Harper & Row.

Gmelch, S. (Eds.). (2004). *Tourists and tourism: A reader.* Long Grove: Waveland Press.

Goodwin, J. (2002). *Price of honor: Muslim women lift the veil of silence on the Islamic world.* New York: Plume.

Gray, K. & Finely-Hervey, J. (2005). Women and entrepreneurship in Morocco: Debunking stereotypes and discerning strategies. *International Entrepreneurship and Management Journal,* 1, 203-217.

Harris, C. & Wilson, E. (2007). Travelling beyond the boundaries of constraint: Women, travel and empowerment. In Pritchard, A., Morgan, N., Ateljevic, I. & Harris, C. (Eds.), *Tourism and gender: Embodiment, sensuality and experience* (pp.235-250). Oxfordshire, UK: CAB International.

Henderson, K.A. (1991). *Dimensions of choice: A qualitative approach to recreation, parks and leisure research.* State College, PA: Venture.

Henderson, K. & Hickerson, B. (2007). Women and leisure: premises and performances uncovered in an integrative review. *Journal of Leisure Research,* 39 (4), 591-610.

Henderson, J.C. (2003). Managing tourism and Islam in peninsular Malaysia. *Tourism Management,* 24, 447-456.

Hjalager, A. & Andersen, S. (2001). Tourism employment: Contingent work or professional career? *Employee Relations,* 23 (2), 115-129.

Howard-Merriam, K. (1990). Guaranteed seats for political representation of women: the Egyptian example. *Women and Politics,* 10 (1), 17-42.

Hutchison, P. & McGill, J. (1992). *Leisure, integration and community.* Concord, Ontario: Leisurability publications.

Inskeep, E. (1994). *National and regional tourism planning: Methodologies and case studies.* London: Routledge.

Jennings, G. (2005). Interviewing: A focus on qualitative techniques. In Ritchie, B., Burns, P. & Palmer, C. (Eds.), *Tourism research methods: Integrating theory with practice* (pp. 99-117). Wallingford: CABI publishing.

Jordan, F. (1997). An occupational hazard? Sex segregation in tourism employment. *Tourism Management,* 18 (8), 525-534.

Jordan, F. & Gibson, H. (2004). Let your data do the talking: Researching the solo travel experiences of British and American women. In Phillimore, J. & Goodson, L. (Eds.), *Qualitative research in tourism: Ontologies, epistemologies and methodologies* (pp. 215-235). Oxon: Routledge.

Kandiyoti, D. (Eds.). (1991). *Women, Islam and the state.* London, UK: Macmillan.

apur, S. (2005, December) Tourism Trends. *Oman Economic Review,* 56, 40-47.

eddie, N. & Baron, B. (Eds.). (1991). *Women in Middle Eastern history: Shifting boundaries in sex and gender.* New Haven: Yale University Press.

eddie, N. (1991). *Introduction.* In Keddie, N. & Baron, B. (Eds.), Women in Middle Eastern history: Shifting boundaries in sex and gender (pp.1-22). New Haven: Yale University Press.

innaird, V., Kothari, U. & Hall, D. (1994). Tourism: Gender perspectives. In Kinnaird, V. & Hall, D. (Eds.), *Tourism: A gender analysis* (pp.1-34). Chichester: John Wiley & Sons.

eontidou, L. (1994). Gender dimensions of tourism in Greece: Employment, sub-cultures and restructuring. In Kinnaird, V. & Hall, D. (Eds.), *Tourism: A gender analysis* (pp. 74-105). Chichester: John Wiley & Sons.

iu, A. & Wall, G. (2006). Planning tourism employment: A developing country perspective. *Tourism Management,* 27, 159-170.

ucas, R. (2004). *Employment relations in the hospitality and tourism industries.* London, UK: Routledge.

Mansfeld, Y. & Winckler, O. (2008). The role of the tourism industry in transforming a rentier to a long-term viable economy: The case of Bahrain. *Current Issues in Tourism,* 11 (3), 1-31.

Mershen, B. (2007). Development of community-based tourism in Oman: Challenges and opportunities. In Daher, R. (Eds.), *Tourism in the Middle East: Continuity, change and transformation* (pp.188-214). Clevedon: Channel View publications.

Miles, R. (2002). Employment and unemployment in Jordan: The importance of the gender system. *World Development,* 30 (3), 413-427.

Moghadam, V. (1992). Patriarchy and the politics of gender in modernizing societies: Iran, Pakistan and Afghanistan. *International Sociology,* 7 (1), 35-53.

Moghadam, V. (1995). The political economy of female employment in the Arab region. In Khoury, N. & Moghadam, V. (Eds.), *Gender and development in the Arab world: Women's economic participation: patterns and policies* (pp.6-34). Helsinki: United Nations University Press.

Moghadam, V. (1998). *Women, work and economic reform in the Middle East and North Africa.* Colorado: Lynne Rienner Publishers.

Moghadam, V. (2003). *Modernizing women: Gender and social change in the Middle East* (2nd ed.). Colorado: Lynne Rienner publishers.

Papps, I. (1992). Women, work and well-being in the Middle East-An outline of the relevant literature. *Journal of Development Studies,* 28 (4), 595-615.

Parry, D. (2005). Women's leisure as resistance to pronatalist ideology. *Journal of Leisure Research,* 37 (2), 133-151.

Patton, M. Q. (1980). *Qualitative evaluation methods.* Beverly Hills, CA: Sage Publications.

Pattullo, P. (1996) *Last resorts: The cost of tourism in the Caribbean.* Kingston: Ian Randle Publishers.

Phillimore, J. (2002). Women, rural tourism employment, and fun (?). In Swain, M. & Momsen, J. (Eds.), *Gender/Tourism/Fun (?)* (pp.75-89). New York: Cognizant Communication Corporation.

Purcell, K. (1996). The relationship between career and job opportunities: Women's employment in the hospitality industry as a microcosm of women's employment. *Women in Management Review,* 11 (5), 17-24.

Purcell, K. (1997). Women employment in UK tourism: Gender roles and labour markets. In Sincliar, M. T. (Eds.), *Gender, work and tourism* (pp. 35-59). London: Routledge.

Raisborough, J. & Bhatti, M. (2007). Women's leisure and auto/biography: Empowerment and resistance in the garden. *Journal of Leisure Research,* 39 (3), 459-476.

Rahman, S., Junankar, P. N. & Mallik, G. (2009). Factors influencing women's empowerment on microcredit borrowers: a case study in Bangladesh. *Journal of the Asia Pacific Economy,* 14 (3), 287-303.

Reinharz, S. & Davidman, L. (1992). *Feminist methods in social research.* Oxford: Oxford University Press.

Ritter, W. (1975). Recreation and tourism in Islam countries. *Ekistics,* 236, 56-59.

Riley, M., Ladkin, A. & Szivas, E. (2002). *Tourism employment: Analysis and planning.* Clevedon: Channel View publications.

Riphenburg, C. (1998). Changing gender relations and the development process in Oman. In Haddad, Y. & Esposito, J. (Eds.), *Islam, gender and social change* (pp.144-168). New York: Oxford University Press.

Sadek, S. (2000). *Doing business and investing in Oman.* Muscat, Oman: Pricewaterhouse Coopers.

Sadi, M. & Henderson, J. (2005). Local versus foreign workers in the hospitality and tourism industry-A Saudi Arabian perspective. *Cornell Hotel and Restaurant Administration Quarterly,* 46 (2), 247-257.

Said, E.W. (1978) *Orientalism.* New York: Pantheon Books.

Said, E.W. (1993). *Culture and imperialism.* New York: A.A. Knopf

Scott, J. (1997). Chances and choices women and tourism in northern Cyprus. In Sinclair, M.T. (Eds.), *Gender, work and tourism* (pp.57-87). London: Routledge.

Seikaly, M. (1994). Women and social change in Bahrain. *International Journal of Middle East Studies,* 26 (3), 415-426.

Shaban, R., Assaad, R. & Al-Qudsi, S. (1995). The challenge of unemployment in the Arab region. *International Labor Review,* 134 (1), 65-81.

Shaw, S. (2001). Conceptualizing resistance: Women's leisure as political practice. *Journal of Leisure Research.*33 (2), 186-201.

Sindiga, I. (1996). International tourism in Kenya and the marginalization of the Waswahili. *Tourism Management,* 17(6), 425-432.

Sinclair, M. T. (1997). *Gender, work and tourism.* London: Routledge.

Small, J. (1999). Memory-work: A method for researching women's tourist experiences. *Tourism Management,* 20, 25-35.

Sonmez, S. (2001). Tourism behind the veil of Islam: Women and development in the Middle East. In Apostolopoulos, Y., Sonmez, S. & Timothy, D. (Eds.), *Women as producers and consumers of tourism in developing regions* (pp.113-142). Westport, CT: Praeger Publishers.

Stockdale, J. E. (1991). Sexual harassment at work. In Firth-Cozens, J. & West, M. A. (Eds.), *Women at work: Psychological and organizational perspectives* (pp.53-65). Philadelphia: Open University Press.

Swain, M. (1993). Women producers of ethnic arts. *Annals of Tourism Research,* 20 (1), 32-51.

Swain, M. (1995). Gender in tourism. *Annals of Tourism Research,* 22 (2), 247-266.

Szivas, E. & Riley, M. (1999). Tourism employment in conditions of economic transition: The case of Hungary. *Annals of tourism research,* 26 (4), 747-771.

Veal, A. (2006). *Research methods for leisure and tourism: A practical guide* (3rd ed.). Harlow: Prentice Hall/Financial Times.

Winckler, O. (2002). The demographic dilemma of the Arab world: The employment aspect. *Journal of Contemporary History,* 37 (4), 617-636.

Winckler, O. (2007). The birth of Oman's tourism industry. *Tourism An International Interdisciplinary Journal,* 55 (2), 221-234.

VDM publishing house ltd.

Scientific Publishing House
offers
free of charge publication

of current academic research papers, Bachelor´s Theses, Master's Theses, Dissertations or Scientific Monographs

If you have written a thesis which satisfies high content as well as formal demands, and you are interested in a remunerated publication of your work, please send an e-mail with some initial information about yourself and your work to *info@vdm-publishing-house.com*.

Our editorial office will get in touch with you shortly.

VDM Publishing House Ltd.
Meldrum Court 17.
Beau Bassin
Mauritius
www.vdm-publishing-house.com